"In this readable yet elegant gem of a book, Fr. Ron Witherup—both priest and scholar—introduces us to the excitement of encountering Jesus Christ and sharing him with others. He does this by showing how the apostle Paul can powerfully guide us to know Christ better and invite others to do the same. This is an enlightening and inspiring book for all Catholics and, in fact, for all Christians."

> —Michael J. Gorman, Ph.D.
> Raymond E. Brown Professor of Biblical Studies and Theology
> St. Mary's Seminary & University, Baltimore

"Fr. Witherup explains the 'New Evangelization' in a clear, inviting, realistic, and challenging manner. Moreover, he does so by incorporating the writings of one of the great evangelizers of all time, the Apostle Paul. What I appreciate most about this book is that Fr. Witherup invites us to gather the fruits of the 'Year of St. Paul' and bring them to bear on one of the central aspects of the 'Year of Faith,' the call to deepen our own commitment to Christ and to give authentic witness to the gospel."

> —Thomas D. Stegman, SJ
> Associate Professor of New Testament
> Professor Ordinarius in the Ecclesiastical Faculty
> Boston College School of Theology and Ministry

"Ronald Witherup provides us with a way to understand the New Evangelization in light of the greatest evangelizer, St. Paul. After explaining what is meant by the New Evangelization, Father Witherup relates it to St. Paul's own understanding of evangelization in order to show readers how they can carry out the New Evangelization today. This is the perfect book for parishes seeking to implement the New Evangelization."

> —Rev. Frank J. Matera, Pastor St. Mary's Church, Connecticut
> Professor Emeritus from Catholic University
> Author of The Sermon on the Mount

"*Saint Paul and the New Evangelization* by Father Ronald Witherup is a clear, concise and compelling study of the Synod on the New Evangelization and its relationship to the great Apostle to the Gentiles, Saint Paul. But it is even more. It is a spirited invitation to be a part of this life-giving work today."

> —Cardinal Donald Wuerl
> Archbishop of Washington

G000078940

Saint Paul and the New Evangelization

Ronald D. Witherup, SS

LITURGICAL PRESS
Collegeville, Minnesota

www.litpress.org

Nihil Obstat: Reverend Robert Harren, *Censor deputatus*
Imprimatur: ✚ Most Reverend John F. Kinney, J.C.D., D.D., Bishop of St. Cloud, Minnesota, May 10, 2013.

Cover design by Ann Blattner
Cover illustration: *Life of Paul* by Donald Jackson in collaboration with Aidan Hart with contributions from Andrew Jamieson. © 2005 *The Saint John's Bible*. Saint John's University, Collegeville, Minnesota, USA. Used with permission. All rights reserved.

Excerpts from documents of the Second Vatican Council are from *Vatican Council II: The Basic Sixteen Documents,* by Austin Flannery, OP © 1996 (Costello Publishing Company, Inc.). Used with permission.

Excerpts from *Instrumentum Laboris* © 2012 Libreria Editrice Vaticana. Used by permission. All rights reserved.

Unless otherwise noted, all Scripture texts in this work are taken from the *New Revised Standard Version Bible* © 1989, Division of Christian Education of the National Council of the Churches of Christ in the United States of America. Used by permission. All rights reserved.

Library of Congress Cataloging-in-Publication Data

Witherup, Ronald D., 1950–
    Saint Paul and the new evangelization / Ronald D. Witherup.
       pages   cm
    ISBN 978-0-8146-3566-7 (pbk. : alk. paper) — ISBN 978-0-8146-3591-9 (ebook)
    1. Evangelistic work—Catholic Church.   2. Paul, the Apostle, Saint. 3. Catholic Church—Doctrines.   I. Title.

BX2347.4.W58   2013
269'.2—dc23   2013010286

To
His Holiness Pope Emeritus Benedict XVI
(Joseph Ratzinger)
In gratitude for eight years of humble service as successor to
Saint Peter
(April 19, 2005–February 28, 2013),
in recognition of the theological legacy he has left
to the church,
and in thanksgiving for the inspiration he has given to
"the new evangelization
for the transmission of the Christian faith."

Contents

Acknowledgments

This book is intended for the average reader who has no particular expertise in Bible or theology. The purpose of the book is to describe the concept of the "new evangelization," which was the subject of an ordinary synod of Catholic bishops held in Rome, October 7–28, 2012, and to connect the main themes of this concept with a familiar figure from the Bible, Saint Paul. Saint Paul is one of the towering figures of evangelization in Christian history. I believe he provides an inspiring model for the new evangelization, which is a long-term task in the church.

No book is an individual enterprise, but in this case, the very idea of it sprang from elsewhere, namely, the staff of Liturgical Press. When they invited me to consider writing such a book, I demurred at first. Then I had a change of heart, mostly because for many years now I have had a burning interest in Saint Paul and his letters. Secondly, I could think of no better figure than Saint Paul to contribute to a *biblically* based conception of evangelization in our day. Thus, despite other commitments and the pressure of time, I accepted this challenge. I trust the reader will find the result both appealing and informative.

I respectfully dedicate this book to His Holiness Pope Emeritus Benedict XVI, who in nearly eight years as pope made a significant impact on the church's life, especially through his humble service and extensive theological publications. As the draft of this book was nearing its completion, he announced his resignation, effective February 28, 2013, by which he became pope (or pontiff) emeritus. This astonishing news obviously took the world by surprise, and it required a few alterations in my text, though the essential content remains the same. Pope Benedict greatly helped to shape the call for a new evangelization, both by his papal writings and by his interventions during the synod. I dedicate this book in gratitude for his Petrine ministry and his theological expertise.

I thank Liturgical Press and its entire staff for the opportunity to write this little book, especially Peter Dwyer, Hans Christoffersen, Andy Edwards, Colleen Stiller, and Michelle Verkuilen. They have produced the book with characteristic efficiency and expertise. I express my gratitude to Mr. Thomas Raszewski and his staff at the Knott Library at St. Mary's Seminary & University in Baltimore, Maryland, for help with obtaining research materials for this project, among others. I also sincerely thank my confrere Father Thomas R. Hurst, SS, for reading the manuscript and offering several insightful suggestions, and I am very grateful to John R. Donahue, SJ, Howard P. Bleichner, SS, and Frederick J. Cwiekowski, SS, for sharing helpful information along the way. Naturally, any weaknesses or errors in the book are mine alone.

R.D.W.
Feast of the Chair of Saint Peter, 2013

Introduction

When Pope Benedict XVI announced a "Year of Paul" to focus on the life, writings, and legacy of this great apostle, most Catholics were perhaps surprised but intrigued. The year was designed ostensibly to celebrate the bi-millennium of the birth of Paul of Tarsus, which was roughly estimated to be between AD 5 and 10. As the year unfolded from June 28, 2008 to June 29, 2009, Catholics all over the world had the opportunity to study Paul's letters, to reflect prayerfully on his teachings, and simply to get better acquainted with this remarkable saint. By most estimates, the year was a great success. There were symposiums, workshops, Bible institutes and study programs, and conferences that focused on Saint Paul, which enabled Catholics to become more knowledgeable about Paul and his writings.

In addition, many bishops, priests, and deacons used the year to preach on Paul's letters, at least occasionally, at Sunday or daily Eucharist. Although large excerpts of Paul's letters appear in the readings of the Mass every liturgical year, it has generally been rare to have preachers focus their homilies on these second readings of Sunday (or first reading on weekdays). Most preachers emphasize the gospel readings, which are geared thematically to the first reading on Sunday. So Paul often got left out. The Year of Paul was one way to correct this little imbalance.

Then four years later, on the eve of the "Year of Faith" proclaimed by Pope Benedict XVI to take place from October 11, 2012 to November 24, 2013, the situation was a bit different. First of all, the notion of "faith" was such a vast and impersonal idea that some people seemingly struggled to get a focus for another thematic year that was so much less personal. Even the intervening thematic "Year for Priests" (2009–10) provided a more concrete focus, a chance to honor faithful priests for their ministry and to celebrate the gift of priesthood to the church.

But another challenge became evident too. The beginning of the Year of Faith was tied to the opening of the thirteenth ordinary synod of bishops (October 7–28, 2012), whose theme was "The New Evangelization for the Transmission of the Christian Faith." The very idea of the "new evangelization" has quite evidently confused many Catholics. What was "new" about evangelization? For that matter, what does evangelization have to do with *me*? Isn't that the job of the priests and bishops, or catechists and theologians?

Various attempts to define or describe in detail the new evangelization have met, at best, with mixed results. Of course, one problem is that the official church documents that discuss or outline the new evangelization are, by and large, not read by the average Catholic. Official documents from the church, in other words, the church's "magisterial" teachings, have a way of being passed over by many Catholics. They are often long, use technical vocabulary or church jargon, or honestly are rather dull for the average person in the pew.

Enter this book! The topic was suggested to me by Liturgical Press because they thought it could provide an entry-point for interested Catholics (and other Christians) to become more familiar with the new evangelization. By reflecting on the theme of the synod through the lens of Saint Paul and his writings, the Press believed more Catholics could "come on board" the new evangelization with an expert guide, Paul the Apostle, as their companion. I ultimately embraced the idea because there is no more quintessential evangelizer in Christian history than Paul. He is the consummate, tireless proclaimer of the Gospel of Jesus Christ. Although he would not be familiar with a concept like the "*new* evangelization," he nevertheless serves well as a resource for this mission in the twenty-first century and the early decades of the third Christian millennium. I believe this offers us an occasion to "kill two birds with one stone," as the saying goes. We can get more familiar with the idea of the new evangelization that was proposed both by Pope John Paul II and Pope Benedict XVI. It can also afford us an opportunity for a review of Paul the Apostle and his significance. Frankly, I find now that the Year of Paul has passed, there is little energy among Catholics for maintaining some of the good practices we began during that year. So Paul seemingly has returned to the background, despite the fact that his concepts have shaped much of the church's teaching that today we recognize as basic tenets of the faith (faith, hope, love, the Eucharist, baptism, the cross, resurrection, etc.).

The goal of this book, then, is to explore the theme of the new evangelization with information that comes both from the official church documents on the theme and pertinent observations from the New Testament letters of Paul. Since the intended audience is the average person in the pew, there are no footnotes or extended treatments of complex ideas. I will attempt as forthrightly as possible to explain the new evangelization and why Saint Paul makes such a good model for it. As much as possible, I will paraphrase some of this information, but I will also cite, as needed, appropriate passages from church documents and Paul's letters.

As an aid to memory, I have provided several charts in the text and appendixes in the back of the book that will summarize important data in a nutshell. These provide a kind of "bird's-eye view" of essential information for our theme. Biblical and magisterial citations will be provided so that more ambitious readers (hope springs eternal!) who wish to pursue the theme on their own may do so reliably at their leisure. Also provided are a glossary of essential terms that can be consulted at will and a short list of recommended resources for further reading.

On June 13, 2013, Pope Francis announced at a meeting with the members of the XIII Ordinary Council the General Secretariat of the Synod of Bishops in Rome that an exhortation from the synod on the new evangelization was nearing completion. He indicated that his predecessor, Pope Benedict, had already begun work on it, and now it is in his hands. Since no date has been set for its release, and since it is still a work in progress, I cannot, unfortunately, include it in this book. At least this announcement clearly indicates that an apostolic exhortation with reference to the synod will be forthcoming. It will doubtless be an important document on the theme of the new evangelization that readers of this book will want to take into account when it becomes available.

To begin, we will first look at some basic vocabulary that relates to synods, since many people (let alone Catholics) are not very familiar with this technical terminology. Then we will begin our study in earnest. We will first address the synod for the new evangelization itself and what we can learn about the nature of the new evangelization. Then we will review some essential information on Saint Paul. The remaining chapters of the book will then bring the two together, attempting to illustrate why this premier apostle is an appropriate model for the new evangelization for the transmission of the faith.

Chapter

1

Synods and
What They Mean

For many people, including Catholics, entering the realm of official teachings of the Catholic Church can be a bit bewildering. Immediately one confronts unfamiliar words, essentially a foreign vocabulary. Not only that, but few recognize the diverse levels of authority contained in Catholic teaching. Not everything is proclaimed on the same level of authority. So while it may seem to be an arcane exercise, there is no easy way to discuss official church documents without knowing some of the terminology, much of which derives from Latin.

The official language of Catholic Church documents is still Latin. Thus many documents are referred to by Latin titles. I do not see a way around this, and when quoting or citing official documents I will use abbreviations deriving from these titles. So let me clarify some of this language here, though the reader can always consult the glossary at the end of the book whenever there is a need to refresh the memory of a definition.

First, we should define a *synod*. A synod is an ecclesiastical term used by various churches for an assembly or a gathering of church officials, either for purposes of consultation or to address timely issues and perhaps create policies, guidelines, or rules to meet these issues. In the Catholic Church, this is a "synod of bishops," though individual dioceses sometimes conduct local synods too.

The synods of bishops are not on the level of an ecumenical council, which is a gathering of the world's bishops and which happens only rarely. In 1965 Pope Paul VI initiated the practice of regular synods of bishops as a way to keep abreast of church issues in the wake of the Second Vatican Council (1962–65). These synods were seen as a means of addressing church matters of universal or regional concern that would not require a "council," which is a rare, extensive, and costly enterprise. (The last ecumenical council before Vatican II was Vatican I, 1868–70, nearly a hundred years earlier! There have only been twenty-one ecumenical councils in history since the church's founding.)

A department of the Holy See called the Synod of Bishops, also established by Pope Paul VI in 1965, prepares and directs the work of synods, under the oversight of a general secretary, who is currently Croatian Archbishop Nicola Eterović. According to Paul VI, the synod's purpose was "to keep alive the spirit of collegiality engendered by the conciliar experience" of Vatican Council II.

Since this foundation, twelve *ordinary* synods of bishops had been held in the Catholic Church prior to 2012, along with numerous special synods, focusing on regions or special themes, such as Africa, Asia, the Netherlands, Europe, Lebanon, the Americas, Oceania, and the Middle East (see appendix A). The synod on the new evangelization for the transmission of the Christian faith was the thirteenth ordinary synod. Although previous synods usually lasted a month, Pope Benedict XVI chose to reduce it to a three-week event. An idea of this particular synod's importance in the mind of the pope was that he had earlier established a Vatican office (also called a dicastery), the Pontifical Council for Promoting the New Evangelization (September 21, 2010). At that time he also named Italian Archbishop Rino Fisichella as its president, and Colombian Archbishop Jose Octavio Ruiz Arenas as its secretary. In conjunction with the General Secretariat of the Synod of Bishops, they helped to prepare the 2012 synod.

The pope calls for a synod and sets the theme and the agenda, but the participants come from around the world. These include:

- the heads of the dicasteries of the Roman Curia, who are usually cardinals;
- delegates elected from the conferences of Catholic bishops;
- patriarchs and major archbishops from the Eastern rite churches;

- a certain number of representatives from religious communities, usually superiors general;
- delegates personally named by the pope.

In addition, certain experts on the chosen theme are appointed by the Holy Father to aid the work of the voting participants. He may also invite some "auditors" or others who represent other denominations not in union with Rome. For the synod on the new evangelization, the pope invited two major figures to address the synod, and they gave memorable presentations: Archbishop Rowan Williams, the outgoing archbishop of Canterbury (representing the Anglican communion), and Ecumenical Patriarch Bartholomew I of Constantinople (representing the Orthodox faith). For this synod, the pope himself attended most of the sessions and gave interventions.

Importantly, the pope also names a group of three or more bishops to oversee the synod: a president-delegate (or often three of them, to alternate duties for presiding at sessions), a general relator, and a special secretary. The general relator's job is particularly important. He must prepare the opening and closing presentations of the synod and oversee the synthesis at the end of the synod, which usually contains the proposals or "propositions" that are then sent to the Holy Father for his consideration.

When a synod of bishops meets there are lengthy preparatory and follow-up processes involved. Synods use certain kinds of specialized documents. The preparatory or preliminary outline document is called the *Lineamenta* (Lin). It is circulated many months in advance to promote discussion among bishops, experts, and laity. (In the case of the new evangelization, the *Lineamenta* was published in February 2011.) The feedback is then compiled by the Roman officials and another document is formulated, a working document for those who will attend the synod. It is called the *Instrumentum Laboris* (IL). For the synod on the new evangelization this working document was published in various languages in June 2012, to allow some months of reflection time in preparation for the synod.

At the conclusion of a synod, there may be a closing statement by the synod fathers, though that is not necessarily true in every case. Eventually, however, the pope usually issues a final document from the synod, an *apostolic exhortation* with a title, often in Latin, summarizing the final teaching from the synod. This can take as long as two years or so to produce, so there will be no such exhortation from the synod on the new evangelization right away. A further complicating factor is the change in popes, which came about after the unexpected resignation of Pope Benedict XVI at the end of February 2013. On July 5, 2013, Pope Francis promulgated his first encyclical letter, *Lumen Fidei* (Light of Faith), a document intended to express major themes in the Year of Faith. He termed it "an encyclical written with four hands, so to speak," because it was begun by his predecessor Pope Benedict XVI and completed by himself. It is treated at some length in appendix E.

The most recent postsynodal apostolic exhortation to be issued was *Verbum Domini* (2010), which contained insights from the twelfth ordinary synod of bishops, on the Word of God (2008). This document is particularly pertinent to our task, since it mentions implicitly and explicitly the role of the Word of God in the new evangelization, something we will address later in this book. The letters of Paul, in particular, form an important resource of Sacred Scripture for all manner of teachings, including those concerning evangelization.

Why are synods important? For some Catholics, synods are probably a distant reality that scarcely enters their worldview. Yet synods are, in fact, an important institution in the Catholic Church since their reemphasis after the Second Vatican Council. Synods provide a vehicle for the pope to consult broadly with representatives of the world's bishops and certain experts on pertinent questions confronting the church today. Synods represent an occasion for collegiality, cooperative consultation especially between the pope and the bishops, for the good of the whole church. It is certainly a cheaper and more efficient vehicle than an ecumenical council. Some experts, however, point out that recent popes have worked to limit the authority of synods. Synods have certainly evolved since the time of Paul VI. They have no power to teach on their own, and even the final documents are now usually prepared by the pope and not issued in the name of the synod participants.

If synods are not well appreciated among Catholics, they have nonetheless had an impact on the church's life, at least to some degree. The synod of 1985, for instance, resulted in some basic principles for an authentic interpretation of the Second Vatican Council itself. An earlier synod in 1971 was also significant because it announced the importance of working for justice in the world, a principle that continues to impact the church's extensive social teaching on justice and peace. Moreover, the 1990 synod on priestly formation ultimately led to John Paul II's apostolic exhortation *Pastores Dabo Vobis* (1992), which not only reshaped priestly formation but also provided a model for other types of ministerial formation in the church. So, at least some synods can have a long-lasting effect in church life.

At least on the level of theory, the 2012 synod of bishops on the new evangelization for the transmission of the Christian faith holds great promise for the church if its vision can be truly implemented and if certain pitfalls can be avoided. This is one reason why I believe it is worth looking at Saint Paul as a model for the new evangelization, for there was never in history a more visionary, wide-ranging evangelizer than "the Apostle."

Review and Reflection Questions

1. How familiar are you with the synods of bishops that have been held since Vatican Council II? Can you name any themes that they have addressed?

2. What is the difference between an "ecumenical council" and a "synod"?

3. What is the difference between a *Lineamenta* and an *Instrumentum Laboris*? Have you read one or the other regarding the synod on the new evangelization, and, if so, how did you react to it?

4. How important do you think the synod on the new evangelization will be for the church? for your parish? for you?

Chapter

2

What Is the
"New Evangelization"?

We begin immediately with the concept of the new evangelization. In fact, the term is a bit slippery and risks being described in so many ways that it can be hard to pin down.

Its roots go back at least to Pope Paul VI in his encyclical *Evangelii Nuntiandi* (1975) in the context of the church's outreach to the modern world. Evangelization, of course, comes from the Greek root "to proclaim good news," and it has been particularly used by Christians in every age to speak of the mission *ad gentes*, that is, the outreach to all peoples in the world to bring them to Christ. Paul VI's encyclical gave renewed energy to the mission of the church always to embrace its call to announce Good News—the Gospel message—to the world, in accordance with Jesus' postresurrectional command to his disciples. Recall the exhortation of Jesus to his disciples at the end of Matthew's gospel:

> And Jesus came and said to them, "All authority in heaven and on earth has been given to me. Go therefore and make disciples of all nations, baptizing them in the name of the Father and of the Son and of the Holy Spirit, and teaching them to obey everything that I have commanded you. And remember, I am with you always, to the end of the age." (Matt 28:18-20; see also Mark 16:15)

As all the gospels show, Jesus' mission was always outwardly oriented. He desired to bring people into contact with his heavenly Father, and he willingly shared his mission with his own disciples. In the wake of the Second Vatican Council, which itself had reached out to the modern world through several of its teachings, Pope Paul VI tried to revitalize this orientation in the church, especially by means of his encyclical.

Later, Pope John Paul II picked up on this theme in numerous contexts. He seems first to have used the expression "new evangelization" during a visit in June 1979 to his home country of Poland, when he went to celebrate Mass in Nova Huta. This was a new suburb near Cracow, where he had been archbishop. It had been built by the Communists, who at that time ruled Poland, as a kind of model for the secular, atheistic society they championed. Originally, the Communists had attempted to prevent Christmas Mass from being celebrated there (1973), but eventually they caved in to the demands of the people. The pope recalled the great witness of the Polish people in this difficult circumstance and went on to proclaim their witness as a "new evangelization," a kind of "second proclamation" or "re-evangelization" of the Gospel in new circumstances.

A few years later Pope John Paul II used the same expression in Haiti in 1983 on the occasion of a meeting of the bishops of Latin America and the Caribbean. In the context of the challenges faced by that region of the world, where both the increase of secularism and the aggressive recruitment of Evangelical Christians among Catholics pose serious threats to the faith, the pope called for a "new evangelization"—not expressed this time as a "re-evangelization"—to further strengthen the Catholic faith under the pressures of modern threats.

Most significantly, John Paul II went on to address the new evangelization in his encyclical letter *Redemptoris Missio* (1990), where he in fact uses both expressions— new evangelization and re-evangelization— almost as synonyms (see 33; IL 13; and *Christifidelis Laici* 34). In this encyclical, the pope distinguishes three groups of people in the modern world. The first group consists of those who have not yet heard or received the message of the Gospel and are in need of a kind of traditional evangelization, the evangelization *ad gentes*. Then there are those who have already received the Christian faith and are solid in its practice. But it is to a third and intermediary group to whom he directs the expression "new evangelization" or "re-evangelization." They are those who once received the message of the Gospel of Jesus Christ but have either grown lukewarm in it or have abandoned it altogether. They need to be fired up again, we might say. There is a need for a dramatic new outreach to this group, which provides the main focus of the new evangelization in this encyclical.

Description of the New Evangelization

But what is this new evangelization?

Before I attempt to define, or rather describe, the new evangelization, I should indicate what it is *not*. It is not a new Gospel message, since the Gospel is always one and the same through history. The truth of the Gospel does not change. Nor is the new evangelization merely a new formulation of an old message. Although new forms of expression are needed, they do not themselves constitute a new evangelization. It is also not simply a warmed-over old evangelization in the sense of a reenergized worldwide mission to proclaim the Gospel of Jesus Christ to the ends of the earth, though this remains part of the church's mission in every era.

The new evangelization has at least six characteristics.

First, it is *personalistic and Christocentric (Christ-centered)*, focused on promoting a personal relationship with Jesus Christ. It is centered on the person of Jesus Christ, who as Savior of the world invites every human being into relationship. Both John Paul II and Benedict XVI repeatedly emphasized faith as a personal encounter with the risen Lord Jesus (also IL 18). An essential aspect of this encounter is the Word of God, for Jesus is none other than the living Word, the Word made flesh. Any outreach, then, is going to involve getting people to encounter the Word of God, and Jesus Christ particularly, in a personal way. This more personal viewpoint moves the new evangelization beyond merely disseminating the content of the faith. The new evangelization is not simply sharing a message or the essential elements of Christianity. It involves an invitation to a personal relationship, first with Christ, and then also with all who embrace Christ as the Savior of the world.

Second, the new evangelization strongly calls for a *rediscovery of the missionary spirit* among all believers. This is essentially a call to rediscover the enthusiasm and outward movement that was characteristic of the first disciples of Jesus, once they were empowered by the Holy Spirit at Pentecost to go forth and preach good news (see Acts 2:1-13). It involves a desire to share the truth of the Gospel message with anyone and everyone who is willing to listen. It also calls for a certain missionary "spirituality" that involves strength, courage, and renewed energy. The bishops of Latin America addressed this theme prominently in their meeting, attended by Pope Benedict XVI, at Aparecida, Brazil (May 13–31, 2007). The final document (2008) issued from that meeting spoke of Catholics needing to become "disciple missionaries" or "missionary disciples" (Aparecida, 2.2.E; 3.A). It also pointed out the role that small faith communities—*communidades de base* in Spanish, that is, small groups of the faithful—play in promoting this transformation (Aparecida, 64.3). Such smaller groups have become important in the context of some of the large Catholic parishes that exist in many parts of the world. Essentially, all the church faithful are asked to reignite this missionary spirit.

Third, the new evangelization is *not merely oriented outwardly* (Latin, *ad extra*) *but inwardly* (Latin, *ad intra*) (IL 76). Of course, the church's mission is always evangelistic, outwardly moving, seeking to take Christ into the missions, especially to areas where the faith is unknown. But the new evangelization is simultaneously inwardly directed to those who already have encountered Jesus Christ but who, for various reasons, may have abandoned their faith or are lukewarm or inattentive to it. In a sense, this is a call to a *re-evangelization* in areas and among people where a prior evangelization has encountered challenges to growth, much like Jesus' parable of the seed (IL 85; see Matt 13:3-8, 18-23). Not all of "the word of the kingdom" (Matt 13:19) fell on good ground! I choose Matthew's rather than Mark's version (cf. Mark 4:8) of this parable for a reason. The declining rather than rising harvest figures are perhaps more realistic in the face of modern challenges to evangelization. In any case, the new evangelization focuses on believers as well as nonbelievers.

The fourth aspect of the new evangelization is that it is *not only targeted to individuals but also to whole cultures* (IL 49, 52). It encompasses an attempt to bring modern cultures into contact with Jesus Christ and to afford them a conversion to the Gospel message. This is a bold enterprise. It entails much more than merely preaching the Gospel to individuals, though this is an ever-present task. To address whole cultures, where the influences of modern, secular societies are so much in evidence, the church must embrace new means of communication and modern methods of promoting social interaction in a way that can transform society itself, making it more the ideal human community it is called to be. Pope Benedict XVI might serve as an example. In late 2012 he started posting "tweets" on Twitter, short 140-character messages that reach out to communications-savvy people around the world, especially the young.

A fifth characteristic is that the task of evangelization is *not merely intended for missionaries, the ordained, or specialists, but for every Christian. It is a task for the entire church.* No one is exempt (IL 89, 92, 118; *Evangelii Nuntiandi* 59). All the baptized are called to the mission of making disciples (Matt 28:16-20)—or, to use the language of the Aparecida document, to become "missionary disciples." Again, in a Catholic context, this is a challenge, as many Catholics are less than enthusiastic about proclaiming their faith publicly, a trait more at home in the Evangelical tradition of Christianity. The *Lineamenta* for the synod stated this point clearly:

> The responsibility of announcing and proclaiming is not the work of a single person or a select few, but a gift given to every person who confidently responds to the call of faith. Nor is transmitting the faith a specialized work assigned to a group of people or specifically designated individuals, but an experience of every Christian and the entire Church. Through this work, the Church continually rediscovers her identity as a People united by the call of the Spirit, who brings us together from the countless areas of everyday living to experience Christ's presence among us and, thereby, to discover God as Father. (Lin 12; also *Verbum Domini* 94; and IL 11)

Finally, the new evangelization *envisions an entire process of Christianization* whereby people engage the risen Lord to such a degree that their whole life changes. Pope Paul VI had already spoken of the "complex process" of evangelization (*Evangelii Nuntiandi* 24), but the situation has hardly become less complex in the twenty-first century. I suggest this vision is very Pauline in conception, since Paul obviously speaks of a "new creation" in relation to his (and others') new life that is found *in* Christ (2 Cor 5:17; Gal 6:15). The goal is a total transformation inward and outward to become the new person in Christ. This process ideally results in a new way of living in accordance with God's will.

These six characteristics are not meant to be comprehensive of the new evangelization, but they do provide an important orientation to the connection with the Word of God. Each of these involves one aspect or another of the Word of God. Thus, we need to return to the Scriptures regularly for inspiration, and Paul's writings are especially a great resource. The task of the new evangelization is also obviously daunting. The real question will be whether or not Catholics, and perhaps other Christians as well, are truly willing to put their faith in action in accordance with this kind of vision. But has this not always been the challenge of faith? That is why a part of the new evangelization involves serious reflection on the transmission of the faith from one generation to the next.

Final Propositions from the Synod

So what did the synod on the new evangelization actually accomplish? Each synod produces some final propositions that summarize the main points that have been agreed upon by the synod participants. The chart below gives a summary of the final propositions issued at the end of the synod on the new evangelization and sent to the Holy Father for his consideration. He authorized their publication and they may be used in the formulation of a final document—perhaps an apostolic exhortation by Pope Francis—on the theme of the new evangelization for the transmission of the faith. For a succinct summary of each of the fifty-eight propositions, see the chart in appendix D.

Outline of the Final Propositions

Section	Propositions
Introduction	1–3
Part One: The Nature of the New Evangelization	4–12
Part Two: The Context of the Church's Ministry Today	13–25
Part Three: Pastoral Responses to the Circumstances of Our Day	26–40
Part Four: Agents/Participants in the New Evangelization	41–56
Conclusion	57–58

One notes the logical outline of this final compilation. After a brief introduction and expressions of gratitude for prior papal teachings on evangelization, the document turns to define or describe the new evangelization. It is interesting to note that this section shows evidence of a slight change in direction that became evident during the synod. Originally, much of the preparatory documentation emphasized the "new evangelization" as directed primarily toward those who have already received the faith but have abandoned or become lukewarm in it. This orientation is still evident in the final propositions, but a renewed emphasis on the mission *ad gentes* or *ad extra*, that is, an outreach to those who have not received the Gospel message, is now also prominent. It reinforces the notion that the church is always on mission, always outwardly oriented to proclaim the message of Jesus Christ.

The second section contains thirteen propositions that explore the many complex facets of the modern world that affect evangelization. The preparatory documents for the synod had in fact expressed many of these concerns. Notably, this section begins by recalling that evangelization "cannot be imposed, but only proposed" (Prop. 13). Religious freedom is a precious human right that must always be safeguarded (Prop. 16). Another interesting point is the comment on the particular complexities of modern urban life (Prop. 25). The new evangelization thus finds itself in the midst of many challenging situations that characterize modern life.

The fifteen propositions that comprise the third section address the multiple pastoral needs that exist in the world today. Unsurprisingly, an emphasis is given to catechetics, the need to teach concretely the Christian faith at all levels of the church. The document even recommends exploring the possible institution of a formal ministry of catechist, such as already exists for deacons, readers, and extraordinary eucharistic ministers. Parishes are also emphasized as the place where so much evangelization can and must take place. Due recognition is given to the *Catechism of the Catholic Church* and its *Compendium* or short summary. Also noteworthy is the call for theologians to make the new evangelization central in their research, and the express desire for increased holiness among all Catholics so that evangelization can be made more effective.

The fourth section, with its sixteen propositions, then addresses the many different agents and participants in the new evangelization. As has become rather prominent in many postsynodal teachings, the various categories of church members are addressed explicitly: the laity, families, bishops, priests, deacons, consecrated religious, seminarians, and youth. Each group has a role to play. Once more the importance of parishes is highlighted, as is the role of the diocesan bishop who is called to be "an evangelizer who leads by example" (Prop. 49). All the baptized are called to participate in the new evangelization with joy, a characteristic of true believers (Prop. 50).

This is also the section where explicit reference is made to the ongoing need for ecumenism, interfaith dialogue, and even conversations with nonbelievers through the forum of "the courtyard of the Gentiles." Pope Benedict XVI promoted this latter image in reference to the ancient practice at the Jerusalem temple, where non-Jews (Gentiles) could still congregate, even though they did not share Israel's faith. The "courtyard of the Gentiles" thus became his favorite image for this encounter with nonbelievers. One proposition also calls for mutual openness between science and faith (Prop. 54), showing the church's basic stance that faith and reason can work together for the good of all humanity.

Finally, the document contains two propositions for a conclusion, one on the need for renewal of faith and the other on seeing Mary as the "model" of evangelization. Building on Pope Paul VI's earlier teaching on evangelization, the document labels Mary "the Star of the New Evangelization" (Prop. 58). She continues to provide a beautiful model for the new evangelization because of her willingness to accept God's Word and humbly implement it in her life (Luke 1:38).

How many of these propositions will be accepted and used by the pope in a final teaching is an open question. As stated earlier, it normally takes nearly two years for such a postsynodal document to appear. We will have to await further direction from Pope Francis, if and when he produces a postsynodal apostolic exhortation. With the appearance of the encyclical *Lumen Fidei*, he has now promulgated a document of his own, based on the prior work of his predecessor, which can impact the long-term project of the new evangelization. In the meantime the new Pontifical Council for Promoting New Evangelization can take this material and work with it in forming concrete plans of action.

Some Cautions

Before moving on to Saint Paul, we need to point out four cautions that relate to the new evangelization. The first caution concerns the use of the terminology "re-evangelization." As mentioned in passing above, not everyone agrees that this is the equivalent of the *new* evangelization. In particular, Archbishop Rino Fisichella, who is the president of the Pontifical Council for Promoting the New Evangelization, has stated his preference to avoid this terminology:

> The problem lies in the prefix "re" and in the multiple meanings it can have. It can express different meanings according to the use to which it is put: it can indicate the repetition of an action, as in the case of re-proposing something; but it can also express the return to a prior phase and an opposing sense, as in reacquiring. ("The New Evangelization: What's it all about?," *America* [October 15, 2012])

The archbishop goes on to give further examples of confusion that can arise from this terminology and defends his preference to avoiding it. This point is a valid one, especially if re-evangelization is taken to mean only repeating what was done in the past. The *Instrumentum Laboris* itself also emphasized the preference for avoidance of the expression "re-evangelization," so that the newness of this enterprise could stand out (IL 45). The new evangelization is not intended to be a repetition of the church's past efforts at evangelization, but something totally new, which reenergizes and redirects the faith for the future.

A second caution concerns the very nature of the new evangelization. There may be a quick desire to reduce it to a set of steps, a program that can be accomplished by a simple series of measures. Cardinal Donald Wuerl, the general relator of the synod, warned against reducing the new evangelization merely to a program. In his final discourse to the synod (the *Relatio post disceptationem*) on October 17, 2012, he recalled that the synod discussions had clearly gone against the notion of a temporary *program* of evangelization:

> Finally, the New Evangelization was recognized as not just a program for the moment but a way of looking at the future of the Church and seeing all of us engaged in inviting, first ourselves to a renewal of the faith and then all those around us into the joyful acceptance of life in the Risen Christ. (Pt. 3; Ques. 11)

This warning basically reminds us that the new evangelization is essentially a process. It involves an invitation to each person, both to those who have already encountered Christ and to those who have not yet heard of him, to accept God's gracious invitation to relationship and to renew the faith over and over again. In a sense, it is a never-ending process, a permanent invitation to ongoing conversion.

A third caution is also in order. As the synod evolved in the course of its three-week session, it seemed to veer more and more into an outward moving direction, with many bishops emphasizing the need to renew efforts to proclaim the Gospel message *ad gentes*, to the world at large. Several speakers, however, called for humility with regard to the new evangelization. The church must be careful not to repeat the errors of the "first" evangelization in which, at times, the church arrogantly proclaimed its superior knowledge and truth in ways that were both detrimental to the faith and impeded the authentic acceptance of faith among those who were offended by this perceived triumphalism. The key to the new evangelization seems to be the witness of the humble lives of those who keep the faith and are willing subsequently to share it. We believers must first accept our own need for ongoing conversion (thus, directed *ad intra*) to sustain the faith in order to give it to others effectively.

Finally, I point to a fourth caution. The *Instrumentum Laboris* outlined in some detail seven "sectors" for the new evangelization to address. These included:

- culture (which was seen as a priority);
- the social sphere (especially recognizing the importance of migration in the modern world);
- the economy;
- civic life (where the church sometimes struggles to have its voice and its ethical teaching heard);
- scientific research and technology;
- communications;
- religion (viewed in a broad sense in light of modern sensitivities where "spirituality" is sometimes defined very loosely).

As you can see from the list, this is an extensive vision indeed to try to address. I believe we will have to work hard not to become too spread out in our efforts at evangelization. While it is true that the church already has many initiatives in each of these sectors, the pace of change in the modern world is enormous. (One needs only to think of the area of communications.) For the church to keep abreast and find appropriate ways to address each of these areas will be a test of both endurance and ingenuity.

With this broad understanding of the new evangelization set forth, in the next chapter we turn to look at how Saint Paul might fit into the vision.

Review and Reflection Questions

1. How many characteristics of the new evangelization can you name and describe?

2. Of the seven sectors targeted in the new evangelization, which ones seem more manageable? What challenges might these hold for the new evangelization?

3. How realistic is the task of the new evangelization for yourself, for your family, and for your parish?

4. How personal is your relationship with Jesus Christ? How would you describe this relationship to others? Do you readily bear witness to this relationship?

3

How Does Saint Paul Relate to the New Evangelization?

If the measure of the relationship of Saint Paul to the new evangelization was determined by the sheer number of biblical citations from his letters in the synod documents, then we would be disappointed. A quick examination of the documents relating to the synod shows that, though Paul is definitely cited on occasion, he is not the centerpiece, except perhaps in the *Instrumentum Laboris*, where he is cited on many different occasions. More frequent citations come from the gospels or other biblical books.

Of course, one cannot minimize the importance of Jesus himself for the origins of evangelization. The gospels clearly portray him as an evangelizer, a man with a mission of proclaiming the kingdom (or reign) of God (e.g., Matt 4:17; Mark 1:14-15; Luke 4:43). Likewise Jesus sent his disciples on mission to evangelize (e.g., Matt 10:5-8; Mark 3:13-15; Luke 9:1-6). Yet the figure that dominates the New Testament in evangelization is Paul.

Think of how Paul is remembered in church history. He was an apostle, a missionary, a preacher and teacher, an evangelizer, a founder of church communities, a letter writer. He was the early church's quintessential convert. Everyone knew the famous story of his conversion, retold three times in the Acts of the Apostles (Acts 9; 22; 26). He had been a violent persecutor of the church, but then through God's grace and the call of the risen Lord on the road to Damascus, he became the church's most ardent promoter.

So why propose Saint Paul as a model for the new evangelization? The reasons are multiple, and the purpose of the remaining chapters of this book is to explain various aspects of Paul's ministry and life that are pertinent to the task of the new evangelization. But first, we need to be sure everyone is "on the same page" with regard to Paul of Tarsus. So I begin by reviewing some basic information about Paul, insofar as scholars can determine it. To that end, I provide a convenient summary chart of Paul's life, so far as it is known, with some key Scripture passages noted in the right-hand column, if you wish to examine the scriptural passages on your own. Then I will provide some brief comments on this information.

Synopsis of the Life of Paul of Tarsus

Event	Date (AD)*	Scripture
Birth in Tarsus in Cilicia (modern Turkey)	5–10	None
Education in Tarsus and Jerusalem Persecution of "the Way"	10–33	Gal 1:13-14; 1 Cor 15:9; Phil 3:6; Acts 8:1-3; 9:1-2
Conversion/commission/call near Damascus	33–35	Gal 1:15-16; Acts 9:1-19
Three years in Arabia (=Nabatea) and Damascus	36–38	Gal 1:17
Short visit to Jerusalem (Two weeks with "pillars" of the church, Cephas and James the brother of the Lord)	35–38	Gal 1:18
Missionary activity in Cilicia, Galatia, Syria, Antioch	37–45	Gal 1:21; Acts 9:30
Paul and Barnabas in Cyprus and Anatolia	45–46	Acts 13:4–14:28
Council of Jerusalem	46–49	Gal 2:1-10; Acts 15:1-21 (see also Acts 11:1-18)

Event	Date (AD)*	Scripture
Span of missionary activity in Asia Minor, Macedonia, etc. *(Period of extant letter writing)*	49–60	Acts 16–20
• Paul and Silas/Silvanus in Macedonia and Achaia: Philippi, Thessalonica, Beroea	49–52	Acts 16:9–18:18
• Sojourn in Corinth (18 mos.)	50–52	Acts 18:1-18
• Sojourn in Ephesus (2 ½–3 yrs.)	52–56	Acts 19:1–20:1
Last visit to Jerusalem; arrest imprisonment in Caesarea (2 yrs.) trial before Festus voyage to Rome	56–59	Acts 21:15–26:32 Acts 23:35–26:32
Imprisonment and preaching in Rome (2 yrs.)	60–63	Acts 28:16-31
Martyrdom in Rome	63–67	None

* All dates are approximate; overlapping is based upon possible conflicting information and flexibility in scholarly reconstruction.

Saul (or Paul) of Tarsus was an Asian. (He likely was known as Saul to his Jewish family and friends, and Paul to the Gentiles, the name by which we remember him; see Acts 13:9.) He was basically a contemporary of Jesus of Nazareth, though he never met him in person except as risen Lord. Jesus was born in the Holy Land roughly between 6 and 4 BC, before the death of Herod the Great, and was crucified around AD 28. Paul was born in Asia Minor (modern Turkey), roughly between AD 5 and 10, in one of the most important cities of the region. Unlike Jesus, Paul was a real city dweller. Tarsus, which Acts calls "an important city" (Acts 21:39), was the capital of the Roman region of the mountainous area of Cilicia, famed for its production of goat-hair tents. Tarsus was located on the Cydnus River and was a prosperous, culturally diverse city of trade.

We know nothing of Paul's immediate family, although Acts mentions his nephew, his sister's son (Acts 23:16). Unlike the first disciples of Jesus, Paul was a Diaspora Jew, that is, one who lived outside of the Holy Land. Though a few scholars maintain that Paul may have been married at one time and had a family of his own, there is no evidence to support this claim. The argument is sometimes made that it was highly unusual for a Jewish male not to be married. True enough, but there were always some exceptions in Judaism, such as Jeremiah the prophet, John the Baptist, and even

Jesus himself. So while celibacy was unusual, it was known at times, and it was usually tied to a special mission given to an individual from God. The biblical evidence shows Paul to be a celibate, like Jesus (see 1 Cor 7:8).

From the very fact of his letters, we can tell that Paul was an educated man. Acts states that Paul was trained by the famous rabbi Gamaliel I (Acts 22:3), but Paul curiously never invokes such a claim when defending himself against opponents who question his background. Yet Paul definitely was familiar with the Jewish Scriptures, most likely in their Greek translation (the Septuagint), which he cites often. His letters show that he was familiar with Jewish practices of scriptural interpretation, as exercised by the rabbis, and also with rhetorical forms from the Greco-Roman world and the Greek philosophical schools of his day. He puts these tools to good use in his letters. He often bolsters his arguments and teachings with effective use of Old Testament biblical quotations or allusions, and with various rhetorical forms.

If we do not know many details of his early life, both Acts and Paul's own letters testify to his firm identity as a Pharisee, a member of this particularly zealous group of lay Jews who strongly desired to preserve and strengthen their Jewish faith. Paul even says that he was more zealous than most of his contemporaries in this regard (Phil 3:6; Gal 1:14; Acts 22:3). This zeal apparently was transferred to his newfound faith after his "conversion"—more appropriately seen as a "call" or "commission" to a new way of life, though I will follow normal convention and use the word "conversion." Paul quickly set off with zeal to proclaim the Gospel of Jesus Christ (Acts 9:20). He never looked back. He never regretted this amazing turnaround in his life. Indeed, he says he counted all his previous life as "rubbish" in comparison to what he had gained in Jesus Christ (Phil 3:8).

Shortly after his 180-degree turn somewhere near Damascus (Syria), Paul went to Arabia (probably Nabatea, to the south and east of the Holy Land) for a mysterious three-year period about which neither he nor Acts tells us anything. This may seem odd until one realizes three things. First, Arabia is associated with another zealous Jew in history, Elijah, who initially fled his enemies but then became a most ardent and effective prophet in his own right. Thus, this action may place Paul in the mold of a prophetic figure, like Elijah. The very language of his divine call near Damascus as expressed in his own words evokes such a prophetic identity (Gal 1:15).

A second factor is that Acts indicates, and for good reason, that Paul was still feared after his conversion (Acts 9:13). He was distrusted. And why not? Such a dramatic change in one who was so forcefully persecuting followers of Jesus, and then who suddenly has a change of heart, must have seemed fanciful at best, dangerous at worst. Was he a spy? Was he feigning conversion in order to compromise these "Christians"? So, going to Nabatea got Paul off the scene, out of danger to himself, and at a guarded distance from those who initially may have doubted the sincerity of this conversion.

I think there is a possible third reason for Paul going to this desert region. Nabatea boasted one of the earliest Christian communities. It could easily have provided a local community to host Paul and, at the same time, to give him further instruction in his newfound faith. The New Testament does not mention this, of course, but we must remember that in his letters Paul sometimes cites what is already significant Christian tradition, especially about Jesus himself. Think of the "Lord's Supper" (1 Cor 11:23-26), the resurrection (1 Cor 15:1-5), or the great Philippians hymn (Phil 2:5-11). The formulation of these passages is based upon pre-Pauline tradition, which Paul *may* well have learned, in part, from those who were sharers in the faith before him. The point is that somewhere along the line, Paul came into contact with what we might call "the Jesus traditions," and I see no reason to think that this did not begin quite quickly after his conversion and baptism.

After this time away, a most amazing thing happened in Paul's life. He says only after being off the scene for a time did he finally go up to Jerusalem, which is where the Christian faith obviously began, to consult with the "pillars" of the church—Peter (= Cephas/Kephas [the Aramaic form of Simon Peter's name]) and James the brother of the Lord (Gal 1:18-19; 2:9). It seems that this consultation was essentially to get the authorities' approval for his special mission. For Paul saw himself as, and indeed was, called by the risen Lord Jesus to be the "apostle to the Gentiles" (Rom 11:13; Acts 9:16). Thus began the most productive and remarkable phase of Paul's life, his ministry as apostle, missionary, evangelizer, and founder of church communities around the ancient Mediterranean basin.

The rest of his life, as indicated in the chart, consists of a series of missionary journeys, letter writing, and ultimately imprisonments and, according to ancient tradition, martyrdom in Rome in the time of the emperor Nero. Note that, even allowing for flexibility in the timeline on the chart, Paul ministered for some thirty years as a missionary. Occasionally, he spent a long time in a given area, such as at Corinth and Ephesus, working for a living by making and selling his tents while constantly engaging in evangelization. Before I comment on what this synopsis of Paul's life and Christianity might mean for the new evangelization, a word about Paul's letters is essential.

Of the twenty-seven books in the New Testament, fully thirteen—nearly half—bear Paul's name. He wrote them over approximately a fifteen-year period, but we know that some letters have been lost to history (Col 4:16). His letters constitute the earliest writings of the New Testament. First Thessalonians is, in fact, the oldest book in the New Testament, being written around AD 51, while Paul was in Corinth.

It is not the sheer number of letters, however, that testify to Paul's influence. All scholars would acknowledge that no single author of the New Testament has had more of an impact on Christian faith and theology than Paul. He is the one who has given Christianity much of the vocabulary of the faith. He is the one who first wrote of the "Gospel" message of Jesus Christ and proclaimed the "truth" of this Gospel. Paul's letters speak to us of the Trinity, of the cross and resurrection, of the salvation achieved once and for all in Christ Jesus, of justification by faith, of grace, of the sacraments (especially baptism, Eucharist, and reconciliation), of the theological virtues of faith, hope, and love, of the demands of Christian ethics, of sustained hope, of the arrival one day of God's kingdom, and so on. In other words, Paul's letters are absolutely foundational documents to the Christian faith. He wrote them, however, as a pastor and church founder desiring to stay in touch with those whom he dearly loved and whom he treated as a spiritual father as well as a fellow Christian.

Of these thirteen letters, we should note that modern scholarship is divided on whether all of them come directly from the "quill" of the Apostle himself. (Note that he often used a scribe to pen his letters, though sometimes he signed them himself [Rom 16:22; Gal 6:11].) As a convenient summary of Paul's letters, I offer the following chart, which is organized somewhat chronologically from the earliest to the latest letter.

Chart of the Origin of Paul's Letters

Letter	Approximate Date (AD)	Provenance
1 Thessalonians	50–51	Corinth
1 Corinthians	54–55	Ephesus
2 Corinthians	55–56	Macedonia
Galatians	54–55	Ephesus or Macedonia
Philippians	56	Ephesus, Rome, or Caesarea
Romans	57–58	Corinth
Philemon	60–61	Ephesus, Rome, or Caesarea
2 Thessalonians	mid-80s (or 51–52 if directly from Paul)	Corinth (?)
Colossians	mid-80s (or 54–56 if directly from Paul)	Rome or Ephesus
Ephesians	mid-90s (or 60–63 if directly from Paul)	Rome (?)
2 Timothy	late 60s or mid- to late 90s (or 61–63 if directly from Paul)	Rome
1 Timothy	late 60s or mid- to late 90s (or 62–64 if directly from Paul)	Macedonia
Titus	late 60s or mid- to late 90s (or 62–64 if directly from Paul)	Asia Minor or Macedonia

What the chart shows us is that seven letters (the first seven on the chart) are accepted universally as undisputedly from Paul: 1 Thessalonians, 1–2 Corinthians, Galatians, Philippians, Romans, and Philemon. The remaining six letters are disputed, though no one would deny that they are in the Pauline tradition and certainly express or build upon Paul's genuine thought. For Catholics, all the letters are of equal value for their spiritual instruction, and since all of them are canonical—found in the canon of Sacred Scripture—they are all to be given the same respect. Nevertheless, based on scholarly hypotheses, the chart shows two possible scenarios of dates for these letters, depending on whether one thinks they were penned during Paul's lifetime or later by a disciple of Paul. Note also that the place whence Paul wrote each letter is not always clear. There is thus some uncertainty in the provenance of each letter. For our purposes in this book, however, all thirteen letters come from the Pauline tradition and can be used appropriately as resource material in proposing Paul as a model for evangelization.

Relating Paul and the New Evangelization

Now to the question at hand: How does Paul relate to the new evangelization? At this stage of the book, I only wish to indicate the general direction of my response to this question. The remaining chapters will flesh out more specific aspects of my response. We begin with the six main elements of the new evangelization as described in the last chapter.

Paul's basic approach to the faith is definitely personalistic and Christocentric, the first characteristic we identified in the new evangelization. Paul insists that he was validly called an apostle by the risen Lord Jesus himself, and that this personal encounter not only gave him his mission to the Gentiles but also bestowed upon him a new identity in Christ. However one characterizes Paul's message, Christ is definitely at its center. We will explore this further in the next chapter.

Paul was most obviously a missionary and evangelizer. His apostolic mission was to proclaim good news primarily to the Gentiles, though I believe he never gave up on his own people, the Jews (see Rom 9–11). The new evangelization has called for a rediscovery of the missionary spirit, so we will explore this theme in chapter 5.

A third characteristic of the new evangelization is its dual inward and outward orientation. This means that the evangelical message is meant as much for believers who have already encountered Christ, and who may or may not have become tepid or nonpracticing in their faith, as well as to outsiders who have perhaps never encountered Christ. Paul made a point of incorporating both aspects into his ministry. This will be the focus of chapter 6.

The fourth characteristic of the new evangelization was its call to all Christians to engage in the task. It is not merely intended for specialists, missionaries, the ordained, or religious. It is a mission for all the baptized. Once more I believe we can see in Paul's understanding of baptism and its implications, as well as the practice of his ministry, that this same perspective is evident in his letters. This will be the focus of chapter 7.

The new evangelization targets not only individuals but also whole cultures. It is a more globally oriented process that is conscious of the broad cultural diversity of the modern world. It is highly communal as well as individual. While Paul's world was vastly different from our own, I believe we can legitimately show that Paul had the same basic orientation toward both individual and communal aspects of evangelization. We will examine this theme in chapter 8.

The sixth and final characteristic I mentioned for the new evangelization was that it views the mission of the church today in terms of an entire process of Christianization. That is to say, it is not merely a once-in-a-lifetime change that then permits us to go about our lives in the same way. Encountering Christ dramatically and profoundly changes our entire lives. If Paul would not be familiar with some of our modern terminology regarding this dramatic change of life, he would nonetheless be comfortable with the notion of Christianization as a whole life change, a never-ending process of transformation until we reach the glories of God's kingdom. We will look at this aspect of Paul and the new evangelization in chapter 9.

To these six characteristics, I believe we can add several others that touch aspects of both the new evangelization and Paul. These will be treated in various places in this book, primarily in chapters 9 and 10: the zeal and urgency of the mission, the individual and communal dimensions of faith, the various means that sustain the faith (especially prayer, the Sacred Scriptures, the sacraments, community life, and a commitment to justice and peace), the importance of giving witness to the faith (even to the point of suffering), and the optimism that accompanies the church's mission because of the work of the Holy Spirit in sustaining evangelization.

So, does Paul have something to teach us about the new evangelization? Indeed! I think these numerous aspects of Paul's theological and pastoral perspective provide great modeling for the new evangelization. So we turn now to explore these themes in more detail.

Review and Reflection Questions

1. Name at least three ways in which Paul can provide a good model for the new evangelization. How attractive do you find these for yourself to engage in the new evangelization?

2. How did Paul come to know Jesus Christ? What did this encounter mean to him, and how did it change him?

3. How important is Saint Paul for Christian faith? Can you name three or more aspects of Paul's letters that have influenced subsequent Christian teachings?

4. How familiar are you with Paul's letters? What do you like best about them? What do you like least?

Chapter

4

Faith as Personal and Christ-Centered

The foundational experience of the Christian faith lies not in memorizing a set of doctrines or learning your catechism, though both of these play a role in clarifying the faith. Faith is first of all a personal experience of a relationship. It is a response to God's invitation to each human being to accept his free and gratuitous love. We will explore this theme here in relationship to both Saint Paul and the new evangelization.

Paul's Experience of Faith

The proper place to begin any discussion of Paul's understanding of faith is his personal encounter of the risen Lord on the road to Damascus. Whether it is seen in light of the narrative description recounted in the Acts of the Apostles or viewed through Paul's own self-description of the event as recorded in his letters, the reality is the same. Christ reached out to "touch" Paul, we might say, and his life was never the same thereafter.

Since it is so familiar to most readers, we begin first with the account of Paul's "conversion" in Acts (9:1-9). The essence of the story is well known. Paul is on his way from Jerusalem to Damascus to continue his persecution of the followers of Jesus of Nazareth, whom Acts calls "the Way." While enroute with some colleagues, Paul is suddenly struck to the ground by a flash of light and hears a voice crying out to him: "Saul, Saul, why do you persecute me?" The text continues with Paul's understandable question:

> "Who are you, Lord?" The reply came, "I am Jesus, whom you are persecuting. But get up and enter the city, and you will be told what you are to do." (9:5-6)

Paul is blinded by this incident and has to be led by the hand into the city, where he is told to meet a believer named Ananias, who is understandably a bit hesitant to meet with this fierce persecutor. But the Lord reassures Ananias and says that he has a special mission for this man: Saul (Paul) will become an instrument to bring the Lord's name to the Gentiles. In other words, he will become an evangelizer. He is consequently baptized and begins his ministry, though not without some opposition.

If the details of the other two accounts in Acts (22:6-16 and 26:12-18) differ somewhat, the heart of the story is always the same. Although these are told as first-person accounts in separate speeches on two different occasions, scholars are agreed that the language is highly Lukan in character. They reflect Paul's personal experience through the theological perspective of Luke-Acts. The centerpiece of this autobiographical story is always unchanging. This is nothing less than an encounter with the risen Lord Jesus Christ. It results in Paul's change of direction 180 degrees. He who formerly persecuted the church with great zeal became its most ardent evangelizer. So fixed is Paul's identity in the Christian tradition that he became known as "*the* Apostle."

If we try to go beyond the text itself and ask questions like what did Paul see, how did the voice sound, what was the experience really like, we would be hard-pressed to find satisfactory answers. Yet Acts is clear. Paul personally encountered the same Jesus of Nazareth who had been crucified a few years before, had died and was buried, was resurrected, and was being experienced now as risen Lord.

Paul's Autobiographical Description

What about Paul's own description of this event in his letters? In this regard we are both fortunate and unfortunate. We are fortunate because there are at least two pertinent texts in Paul that speak of this event. Yet we are left hanging somewhat because the language is a bit obscure, and we do not get the clarity we modern people might like.

The most important testimony of Paul's experience is found in his letter to the Galatians. In a fairly long biographical section, Paul recounts his conversion experience in this way:

> But when God, who had set me apart before I was born and called me through his grace, was pleased to reveal his Son to me, so that I might proclaim him among the Gentiles, I did not confer with any human being . . . (Gal 1:15-16)

Notice that this is the language of revelation. Revelation by its very nature is mysterious. It is beyond human control or full comprehension, yet is as real as anything we can concretely feel. Paul also uses vocabulary that is at home in the call of some Old Testament prophets, like Ezekiel or Jeremiah, who speak of their being designated already from the womb. For Paul, the most important aspect of this experience was that it was personal, it was from God, it was an act of pure grace, and it led to his divinely appointed and apostolic mission to the Gentiles. Paul gives us no further details. God revealed Jesus Christ to him and this revelation transformed his life dramatically.

Paul does, however, speak of the same event in different words in another letter, First Corinthians. In the context of recalling the tradition about Christ's death and resurrection, which by Paul's day is already a firm Christian belief, Paul lists a series of postresurrection appearances. This includes such famous personalities as Cephas (Simon Peter) and James, but then he adds a personal note:

> Last of all, as to one untimely born, he appeared also to me. For I am the least of the apostles, unfit to be called an apostle, because I persecuted the church of God. But by the grace of God I am what I am, and his grace toward me has not been in vain. (1 Cor 15:8-10)

Although here Paul uses the language of "appearance" rather than revelation, it gets us no further inside Paul's experience concretely. He does not describe in detail the experience of this "appearance" of the risen Lord.

What is striking, however, is that Paul counts this personal appearance by the risen Lord as exceptional (he is *not* one of the twelve apostles, Jesus' earthly companions), it is effected by grace (God's gracious action), and it has not been in vain (because in fact he became a foremost "apostle" and evangelizer). The personal nature of this experience is simply undeniable.

From our perspective two thousand years later, I think it should also be comforting. It means that being an "apostle"—one sent on a mission— and being able to experience the risen Lord personally is as possible in our day as it was in Paul's. One does not need to have walked with Jesus in ancient Galilee to become his disciple, to be one of his "apostles." While Paul sometimes has to defend his apostolic call rather forcefully, he never relinquishes this identity. The reason is clear—because he received it from the risen Lord himself.

At this point, we might ask whether the language of personal experience is not more at home in an Evangelical Christian environment than in the Catholic Church. In my experience, we Catholics are somewhat hesitant to tout our faith in such personal terms, except perhaps among charismatic groups. Moreover, we rightly insist that the experience of faith is more than merely personal. Faith is not simply a Jesus-and-me reality. There is always a communal dimension to faith, as well as the call to personal faith. (We will explore this aspect in chapter 8.) Yet Paul's testimony assures us that there is always a personal dimension to faith as well. God, in Christ, reaches out to each and every person to invite us to fellowship.

Elsewhere Paul uses such personal language in a rather startling way:

> For through the law I died to the law, so that I might live to God.
> I have been crucified with Christ; and it is no longer I who live,
> but it is Christ who lives in me. And the life I now live in the flesh
> I live by faith in the Son of God, who loved me and gave himself
> for me. (Gal 2:19-20)

This is personal testimony indeed. So transformed was Paul by this experience that he says it is no longer he who lives but really it is Christ who lives in him! This truly makes Christ the centerpiece of his faith. Christ is at work in Paul's very being. Moreover, Paul rejoices in the love that he has received from Christ. He speaks eloquently of "the Son of God, who loved me and gave himself for me." This is the kind of experience of love that is obviously comforting and reassuring. But Paul did not have a simplistic view of what receiving this love demanded of him. For love freely given demands a free response.

The Perspective of Faith

This is where we need to add a word about *faith*. For most Christians today, faith probably evokes a set of doctrines or dogmas to which one assents. It has become for us a very mental or cerebral reality. The Creed, for example, which we recite every Sunday, provides a wonderful summary of the Christian faith, expressed in deeply theological and philosophical language. But for Paul, faith is not just a sum of doctrines. It is more like a verb than a noun. Faith is a trusting relationship. It is active and alive. It begins in God's outstretched hand of friendship, which invites us to respond freely and generously with all our being. Yes, there are doctrinal aspects to faith; faith has specific content. The Pastoral Epistles of Paul (1–2 Timothy, Titus), in particular, show that already in the New Testament there is concern for the content ("deposit") of faith. It is not some vague reality.

We would, however, miss Paul's most fundamental lesson if we only emphasized this point or too quickly reverted to it. Paul's basic teaching on faith is that it is a relationship rooted in trust, which is why he so frequently invokes the image of Abraham, the Jewish patriarch, as the perfect model of faith. To God's mysterious and unexplainable request to relocate his family and enter into covenant with God, Abraham simply does it. No questions asked, no ifs or buts, no delays or hesitation. Abraham trusted God, and so it was that God "reckoned [it] to him as righteousness" (Rom 4:3). For Paul, this is the essence of the faithful response. Abraham accepted God's invitation to a covenantal relationship. In Jesus Christ, we are now invited into a new and eternal covenantal relationship, and this is the essence of our faith.

New Creation and Transformation

One more element of Paul's experience of faith in Jesus Christ needs to be added. Paul makes it clear in his letter to the Philippians that he had once been quite content, even confidently self-satisfied, in his pre-Christian life as a Pharisee. He was always known to be a zealous man, one whose commitments, once made, did not waiver. Yet he testifies to the transformation that he experienced through his new life *in* Christ. Paul defends his credentials as an apostle:

> If anyone else has reason to be confident in the flesh, I have more: circumcised on the eighth day, a member of the people of Israel, of the tribe of Benjamin, a Hebrew born of Hebrews; as to the law, a Pharisee; as to zeal, a persecutor of the church; as to righteousness under the law, blameless. Yet whatever gains I had, these I have come to regard as loss because of Christ. More than that, I regard everything as loss because of the surpassing value of knowing Christ Jesus my Lord. For his sake I have suffered the loss of all things, and I regard them as rubbish, in order that I may gain Christ and be found in him, not having a righteousness of my own that comes from the law, but one that comes through faith in Christ, the righteousness from God based on faith. (Phil 3:4-9)

These are strong words from a former Pharisee. Everything else is "rubbish" (a particularly harsh word in the original Greek) compared to what he has gained in Christ! Such is the remarkable transformation that comes from genuine faith. Joining Christ makes one a new person, gives one a whole new perspective or outlook.

In fact, I believe that in this connection, we can invoke another beautiful Pauline expression, "new creation." It is used only twice in Paul's letters (2 Cor 5:17; Gal 6:15), yet we can consider it an omnipresent undercurrent in Paul's thought. It recalls the dramatic and complete transformation that comes to those who join themselves to Christ, that is, who accept Christ's invitation to faith. Paul says it most clearly in Second Corinthians: "So if anyone is in Christ, there is a new creation: everything old has passed away; see, everything has become new!" (2 Cor 5:17). These words are said in the context of the message of reconciliation that comes from Christ, but I think the sense of the phrase applies to the whole of Paul's thought. Accepting baptism, through which one joins oneself to Christ through water and the Holy Spirit, means accepting God's invitation to new birth in his Son, Jesus Christ. It is another act of creation. It is grace in action, transforming all those who allow themselves to be touched by the love of Christ.

In sum, then, Paul's understanding of the personal and Christ-centered nature of the Christian call to discipleship is a crucial aspect of his own understanding of faith.

The Personal and Christ-Centered Dimension of the New Evangelization

Now, I said in chapter 2 that the new evangelization was both personal and Christ-centered (Christocentric). But here I would like to give a few citations from specific magisterial documents to illustrate this assertion.

Paul shows us that this is not a new perspective. It is, however, an essential aspect of the new evangelization because proclaiming the Christian faith, especially in our day, demands a personal dimension. Christ is still calling apostles to follow him. The risen Christ still reaches out from on high to tap people, often unexpectedly, on the shoulder or whisper in their ear, "Come, follow me." Several texts related to the new evangelization speak to this personal, Christ-centered dimension.

In his very first encyclical letter after his election as pope, Benedict XVI wrote,

> Being Christian is not the result of an ethical choice or a lofty idea, but the encounter with an event, a person, which gives life a new horizon and a decisive direction. . . . Since God has first loved us (cf. 1 Jn 4:10), love is now no longer a mere "command"; it is the response to the gift of love with which God draws near to us. (*Deus Caritas Est* 1)

Pope Benedict XVI, of course, was already relying on other church teaching regarding the personal dimension of God's loving outreach to humanity. Already Vatican Council II's profound document *Dei Verbum*, the Dogmatic Constitution on Divine Revelation (1965), had emphasized the personal dimension to divine revelation that had largely been obscured for several hundred years in the wake of the Protestant Reformation. *Dei Verbum* restored the Catholic understanding of the personal nature of divine revelation as an action of the loving God reaching out in friendship to fallen humanity (DV1). Revelation is first of all a personal call that demands a response; only secondarily does it require more specificity, a wrestling with the mystery of how God reached out to humanity by sending his own Son into the world to suffer, die, rise, and be glorified, and to invite disciples to join in his worldwide mission.

The working document of the synod on the new evangelization itself highlighted this personal dimension of the faith:

> The Christian faith is a true encounter and relationship with Jesus Christ. Transmitting the faith means to create in every place and time the conditions which lead to this encounter between the person and Jesus Christ. The goal of all evangelization is to create the possibility for this encounter, which is, at one and the same time, intimate, personal, public and communal. (IL 18; see also *Catechesi Tradendae* 5)

One notes in this instance, as elsewhere in the documentation for the new evangelization (Prop. 26), that there are multiple dimensions to this personal relationship. It is intimate and private yet also communal and public. Also, the new evangelization demands a pastoral response that takes this into account: "Every pastoral program must transmit the true novelty of the Gospel, and be centered on a personal and living encounter with Jesus" (Prop. 42). It "calls all believers to renew their faith and their personal encounter with Jesus in the Church, to deepen their appreciation of the truth of the faith and joyfully to share it" (Prop. 57).

Cardinal Wuerl, the general relator of the synod, had also signaled the importance of this personal dimension several times in his final presentation at the end of the synod. He underlines the spiritual needs of our age:

> The overriding need of this age is a spiritual renewal that is the task of the Church to proclaim and effect. Spiritual renewal is the most important element of the New Evangelization insofar as it involves the renewal of a personal encounter with Jesus Christ and a catechesis that fosters our spiritual growth. (*Relatio post disceptationem*, Pt. 3; also Q. 6)

This is an acknowledgment that the personal dimension we have been talking about all along is actually at the heart of authentic spirituality. Our human call to holiness, to reflect here on earth our Creator in heaven, is a call to live the life of the triune God—Father, Son, and Holy Spirit—with as much love and commitment as we can muster. This personal call is not diminished by time or conditioned by our periodic and temporary failures to live the life we are called to live. The call to become a disciple, actually an apostle sent on mission, is eternal. The new evangelization invites us to take up this invitation again.

Pope Benedict XVI also addresses this personal dimension in his apostolic exhortation *Verbum Domini* that grew out of the previous synod on the Word of God (2008):

> In stressing faith's intrinsic summons to an ever deeper relationship with Christ, the word of God in our midst, the Synod also emphasized that this word calls each one of us personally, revealing that *life itself is a vocation* from God. In other words, the more we grow in our personal relationship with the Lord Jesus, the more we realize that he is calling us to holiness in and through the definitive choices by which we respond to his love in our lives, taking up tasks and ministries which help to build up the Church. (77)

Here the connection between the personal call and our own mission is intertwined. Our vocation (from the Latin for "call") is to grow closer and closer to the Lord, to accept his gracious invitation to holiness that is both personal and communal. Our common vocation to holiness is lived out in varied ways, as diverse as the ministries in the church itself. But we cannot be effective if we do not respond, and we cannot respond if we do not hear this call and accept it for the free invitation it is.

A brief word is also in order about "the transmission of the Christian faith." This expression formed part of the essential description of the synod, and it also provided a focus for the Year of Faith that began at the inauguration of the synod. Transmitting the faith can, of course, mean several things. Preaching, teaching, catechizing are all formal means of transmitting the faith, that is, sharing it with others. These are largely intellectual communications, pointed explanations of the faith. I believe, however, the intention behind the new evangelization involves more than this, as important as these ongoing activities are in the church. Transmitting the faith is also about sharing our personal relationship with Christ. It requires showing our faith to others. It is about sharing the love that we have received from God with others. One can only transmit this faith if it is, in fact, evident in our lives. So, personal transformation is also a part of this vision. The witness of our lives, lived in accordance with the new covenant of Jesus Christ, is as essential as verbally communicating the faith we have received.

I believe Saint Paul would be at home in this enterprise because it begins with this intense personal relationship with Jesus Christ that sustained him throughout his entire ministry. He was willing to give up everything to possess Christ and to carry him forth to the Gentiles. Now we are invited to follow that same lead and carry him forth in our world. But it involves many more aspects, to which we can now turn in subsequent chapters.

Review and Reflection Questions

1. In what ways is "faith" personal? How would you describe your personal faith?

2. What do you make of Paul's strong language of the evaluation of his pre-Christian life? Do you think he is too harsh in his judgment?

3. Can you identify any ways in which your life of faith has helped you become a "new creation"? Has faith allowed you to see the world in a new way?

4. When you reflect on Jesus Christ in your life, how do you describe your experience of his presence? How personal is this experience of the risen Christ?

The Church's Mission: Evangelization and the Transmission of the Faith

The first paragraph of Vatican Council II's Decree on the Church's Missionary Activity (*Ad Gentes Divinitus*) states clearly and succinctly the reason for the church's existence:

> Having been sent by God to the nations to be "the universal sacrament of salvation," the church, in obedience to the command of her founder (Mt 16:15) and because it is demanded by her own essential universality, strives to preach the gospel to all. The apostles, on whom the church was founded, following the footsteps of Christ "preached the word of truth and brought churches to birth." It is the duty of their successors to carry on this work so that "the word of God may speed on and triumph" (2 Thess 3:1), and the kingdom of God be proclaimed and renewed throughout the whole world. (1; see also *Catechism of the Catholic Church* 849–50)

The church, by its very nature, is mission oriented. Recall that one of the four marks of the church is apostolic (the other three being one, holy, and catholic). This means both that it is founded on the sure foundation of the apostles and that it is sent on mission, for the root meaning of apostle/apostolic is "one who is sent."

All the documentation concerning the new evangelization speaks at length about this evangelistic reality. Evangelizing, spreading the good news of Jesus Christ, is not merely an option. It is an obligation rooted in the church's identity.

Roots of the New Evangelization

We begin, neither with Paul nor with the church's official documents, but with Jesus Christ himself. As I briefly indicated in chapter 3, all the gospels, especially the Synoptic Gospels (Matthew, Mark, Luke), portray Jesus as a man who evangelized from the very beginning of his public ministry. After Jesus' baptism by John the Baptist and John's own arrest, Mark's gospel succinctly summarizes Jesus' mission:

> Now after John was arrested, Jesus came to Galilee, proclaiming the good news of God, and saying, "The time is fulfilled, and the kingdom of God has come near; repent, and believe in the good news." (Mark 1:14-15)

The testimony of all the gospels is that a large part of Jesus' ministry was proclaiming this good news—in short, evangelizing. Jesus concerned himself with calling people to repentance and to proclaiming that God had good news in store for all people. But, simultaneously, Jesus' message involved a call to faith. He called people to *believe* in the good news, and when he sent out his own chosen disciples, his "apostles," he sent them forth to carry on his own mission. The apostles were sent to bear the same message and to share the faith that they had received (Mark 3:13-14; Matt 10:5-8).

If we look elsewhere in the New Testament, we see an even clearer image of the continuity between this Gospel mission of Jesus and the church. Luke-Acts is the only two-volume work in the New Testament. They are also the only books that contain an explicit rationale expressed in their related prefaces (see Luke 1:1-4 and Acts 1:1-5). These brief passages tell us that the story of Jesus of Nazareth continues, by design, in the church's own story. As Jesus preached, taught, proclaimed, healed, and brought people to faith, so the church does likewise. Jesus bestowed upon the church a missionary identity. His call brought people into a community of faith who, in turn, were charged with carrying on the same mission he had received from his heavenly Father. That is why the church has no choice but to remain evangelistic.

Unlike Judaism in general, Christianity is from its roots an outwardly oriented, evangelical religion. The faith that has been received is intended to be shared with others. All disciples share in Jesus' own mission. Faith is not something that one keeps to oneself. Like love, it demands to be shared. That is why an essential part of the church's evangelical mission is transmitting the faith.

Paul's Evangelistic Outlook

Although the gospels were written after Paul's own letters, based upon oral and written traditions about Jesus of Nazareth that circulated in the early church, Paul is the one who essentially gives us the orientation we see in describing the church's evangelical mission. We will focus on five different aspects that connect Paul with the new evangelization.

Apostle, Called and Sent

The first and most evident aspect lies in Paul's own identity as an apostle. He was called and sent by the risen Lord Jesus to become an apostle. Or, to be more accurate, not just *an* apostle but, in fact, *the* Apostle (capital A). The importance of this identity cannot be overestimated. We note, for example, that Paul begins many of his letters by recalling his apostolic "ID." Romans, Paul's most renowned letter, begins with the following words:

> Paul, a servant of Jesus Christ, called to be an apostle, set apart for the gospel of God . . . (Rom 1:1; see also 1 Cor 1:1; 2 Cor 1:1; Gal 1:1)

For Paul, there is no better designation for his Christian identity than to say he is an apostle, one sent by Jesus Christ himself on an evangelical mission to proclaim the Gospel message, which he also calls the "gospel of Christ" (1 Cor 9:12; Gal 1:7) and whose truth he is unwilling to compromise (Gal 2:5, 14).

What makes this apostolic identity so interesting is that it came to Paul not by virtue of being a physical companion of Jesus of Nazareth but because of the personal call he received on the road to Damascus. In fact, Paul has to defend his apostolic identity rather often, and he does so with force. For example, when he describes his call in First Corinthians, he includes himself last, but not least, in the list of apostles:

> Last of all, as to one untimely born, he appeared also to me. For I am the least of the apostles, unfit to be called an apostle, because I persecuted the church of God. But by the grace of God I am what I am, and his grace toward me has not been in vain. On the contrary, I worked harder than any of them—though it was not I, but the grace of God that is with me. Whether then it was I or they, so we proclaim and so you have come to believe. (1 Cor 15:8-11)

Notice in this passage that Paul is at one and the same time proud and humble. He is proud of his apostolic call, which is as genuine as that of any of the prior apostles, but he also recognizes that it is not Paul himself who makes the ministry that comes from this call effective. Rather it is God's "grace" at work in and through him that makes his ministry effective. The point is not which apostle does the proclaiming. More important is that people come to faith through the apostolic ministry.

Throughout his letters Paul makes it clear that this is what he is all about. His mission as an apostle is to spread the good news of Jesus Christ, to proclaim the salvation that comes to all humanity through this same Jesus Christ who is ultimately the Savior of the world (Phil 3:20).

If we ask exactly the nature of Paul's evangelistic activity, the answers would be somewhat diverse. The Acts of the Apostles clearly shows Paul, along with other apostles, engaging in preaching, teaching, and healing ministries. We should note that there is some distinction in the New Testament between preaching (kerygma), which is the oral proclamation of the Gospel message, and teaching (didache), which is more formally instructing people in the faith. We can also recognize a certain level of catechesis, organized instruction of converts, which would have been characteristic of Paul's ministry too. All three of these activities are interrelated and somewhat overlapping. All involve a certain amount of oral proclamation and contributed over time to the development of a body of teachings that form the core of the Christian faith.

The Necessity of Evangelization

A second aspect of Paul's apostolic ministry is his explanation of why it is really necessary. For instance, when he writes to the Romans, a community that he had not founded but with whom he wants to share some of his own thoughts about the faith, he lays out what might be deemed the most explicit rationale for evangelization. Using several passages from the Old Testament, Paul explains the necessity of bringing people to faith:

> The scripture says, "No one who believes in him will be put to shame." For there is no distinction between Jew and Greek; the same Lord is Lord of all and is generous to all who call on him. For, "Everyone who calls on the name of the Lord shall be saved." But how are they to call on one in whom they have not believed? And how are they to believe in one of whom they have never heard? And how are they to hear without someone to proclaim him? And how are they to proclaim him unless they are sent? As it is written, "How beautiful are the feet of those who bring good news!" (Rom 10:11-15)

What Paul is getting at here is that people do not arrive at the Christian faith without being introduced to it. One must encounter the risen Christ to come to know him. And one cannot call upon Christ if they have no familiarity with him. Using the dual designation of Gentile or Jew, which essentially represented for Paul the two primary poles of personal human identity in his day, he says faith is intended for all. But someone must bring the message to these people. Evangelizers—bringers of good news—are thus essential.

Zeal for Evangelization

A third aspect is the urgency of evangelization and the zeal with which Paul embraced his apostolic ministry of evangelizing. While he may have been zealous for his earlier Pharisaic beliefs (Phil 3:6), he nevertheless turned that zeal to evangelizing his newfound faith after his call as an apostle. In a passage that Pope Benedict XVI cited on numerous occasions, and that is picked up in the Final Message of the synod on the new evangelization, Paul says,

> If I proclaim the gospel, this gives me no ground for boasting, for an obligation is laid on me, and woe to me if I do not proclaim the gospel! (1 Cor 9:16)

This is a powerful statement. Paul indicates that his apostolic mission is an obligation that he has received. He is compelled to evangelize, and he does so enthusiastically. He speaks immediately after this line of a "stewardship" or a "commission" he has received. He has been entrusted with something very precious. And he cries out, "woe to me if I do not proclaim the gospel!"

The unmistakable sense of urgency this passage shows is picked up elsewhere in Paul. Near the beginning of Romans, for instance, Paul explains that, though he had been delayed in his intention to visit the Roman community, he felt the urge to do so in fulfillment of his desire to see that all get the message:

> I am [under obligation] both to Greeks and to barbarians, both to the wise and to the foolish—hence my eagerness to proclaim the gospel to you also who are in Rome. (Rom 1:14-15)

Although Paul normally restricted his ministerial outreach to areas where the Gospel had not yet been proclaimed, he did occasionally visit communities where the faith was already established, as in Rome. In this case, Rome was also intended to serve as a stepping-stone to a further mission to Spain (Rom 15:24, 28), though his subsequent imprisonment and martyrdom prevented this. Such visits, however, gave Paul a chance to share his own convictions and understanding of the faith with others. It also afforded him occasion to encounter others, whether Greek or barbarian, whether wise or foolish, with whom he could share his message.

Another passage from Paul that has been frequently cited in the context of the new evangelization expresses the urgency in terms of Christ's love that impels us to go forward. In the midst of his profound passage on reconciliation, Paul writes, "For the love of Christ urges us on . . ." (2 Cor 5:14). This passage is often cited in its Latin (Vulgate) version: *Caritas Christi urget nos . . .* It is the love of Christ that impels us to proclaim the good news of salvation. It is the love of Christ that sustains us on this mission.

The Cross of Christ

A fourth aspect of Paul's evangelization efforts involves the content of his message. Paul did not see himself simply sent to disseminate some vague message of "love" or "well-being." For Paul, there was indeed *content* to his message. It primarily concerned the cross of Christ and the necessity of suffering for the sake of the Gospel message. At times, he clearly faced opposition to his message. It is not an easy message to swallow. Perhaps Paul addresses this issue most clearly at the beginning of his first letter to the Corinthians. In the context of a very divided community, in which people had split into camps, following various leaders in whom they held great confidence, Paul reminds them of the difficulty of evangelizing:

> For Christ did not send me to baptize but to proclaim the gospel, and not with eloquent wisdom, so that the cross of Christ might not be emptied of its power. For the message about the cross is foolishness to those who are perishing, but to us who are being saved it is the power of God. (1 Cor 1:17-18)

In essence, this was Paul's message. He preached Christ crucified and risen from the dead! But this message was at times mocked and at other times rejected outrightly (see Acts 17:32-34). Paul is quite explicit in recalling the fierce opposition he experienced in trying to get this message out. A few lines later in the same chapter, he says,

> For Jews demand signs and Greeks desire wisdom, but we proclaim Christ crucified, a stumbling block to Jews and foolishness to Gentiles, but to those who are the called, both Jews and Greeks, Christ the power of God and the wisdom of God. (1 Cor 1:22-24)

Here is the rub. In Paul's day, Jews looked for "signs" and in fact put their trust in God's law (the Torah), whereas Greeks looked to philosophy (literally, "love of wisdom") for truth and guidance. Paul's message of salvation in Jesus Christ did not fit neatly into either of these categories. Indeed, the Gospel message is an utter paradox. The cross, far from being the image of ignominious defeat and humiliation accorded it in the Greco-Roman world of Paul's day, was a Christian sign of victory. For this reason, Paul notes that his message is perceived as either a stumbling block or absolute foolishness. One wonders if the Christian message is perceived any differently today, in the context of worldly values that seem so much more attractive to some!

The message of Jesus Christ is intimately bound to the cross. There can be no ultimate victory over sin and death without this sacrifice. Paul is insistent to his communities that they stay true to this unsettling message. In purely human terms, the message of the cross is certainly foolish. In a world where might, power, wealth, influence, and success define human existence, the notion that Christian life involves self-sacrifice, suffering, and following Jesus on a path that includes accepting the "cross" seems foolish indeed. Paul says, however, that his strength comes from weakness (2 Cor 12:10).

The Christian message thus has always had a hard time being accepted universally. Paul sometimes was chased out of locations he tried to evangelize. At other times, he was simply ignored or scoffed at. But he never gave up. He never changed the message to suit the audience's desire for quick, slick, or easy answers. The language of love, Paul knew, is rooted in self-sacrifice and the embrace of the cross and resurrection of Christ. To preach the faith in any other fashion would be to empty it of its value (1 Cor 1:17; Gal 1:6-7).

The Holy Spirit as Guide

A fifth and final aspect to which I draw attention is Paul's confidence in the guidance of the Holy Spirit in his mission of evangelization. The same can be said for the new evangelization. While it is true to say that Paul and his companions were courageous in their proclamation of the Gospel message, he would be the first to say it was the gift of the Holy Spirit enabling them to boldly continue their apostolic mission, often in the face of grave dangers. No passage speaks more confidently of Paul's reliance on the Holy Spirit than Romans 8. There Paul asserts that the Holy Spirit helps us in our weakness and that, in the end, nothing can separate us from the love of Christ (esp. verses 38-39).

Elsewhere Paul catalogs his sufferings as an apostle. For the sake of his apostolic mission, he and his companions underwent many trials and tribulations. In one passage, he likens his ministry to a fragile earthen vessel:

> But we have this treasure in clay jars, so that it may be made clear
> that this extraordinary power belongs to God and does not come
> from us. We are afflicted in every way, but not crushed; perplexed,

> but not driven to despair; persecuted, but not forsaken; struck
> down, but not destroyed; always carrying in the body the death
> of Jesus, so that the life of Jesus may also be made visible in our
> bodies. (2 Cor 4:7-10; see also 2 Cor 11:21b-33)

What gives Paul this confidence? He says it himself: it is God's grace at
work in him that can accomplish all the good he can do in the face of many
challenges. It is the power of the Spirit at work in him that provides the
impetus, gives the assurance, produces the results. Essentially, we might
say this is in fact a humble view of the apostolic mission of the church.
It is not an arrogant or triumphal vision, but a humble one, centered on
staying faithful to the cross of Christ even when the odds are against us.

The Perspective of the New Evangelization

Without desiring to belabor the point, I think one can say Paul's approach to his apostolic mission, implicitly and explicitly (seen in the five
features above), permeates many of the documents related to the new
evangelization, especially in the *Instrumentum Laboris*. Let me cite just
a few instances.

In the Final Message of the synod, issued on October 26, 2012, the
text proclaims the following about the new evangelization:

> It is not about starting again, but entering into the long path of
> proclaiming the Gospel with the apostolic courage of Paul who
> would go so far as to say "Woe to me if I do not preach the Gos-
> pel!" (1 Cor 9:16). Throughout history, from the first centuries of
> the Christian era to the present, the Gospel has edified communi-
> ties of believers in all parts of the world. Whether small or great,
> these are the fruit of the dedication of generations of witnesses
> to Jesus—missionaries and martyrs—whom we remember with
> gratitude. (Final Message 2)

Then, in addition to this reminder of the urgency of the mission, the
document warns of challenges:

> We are not intimidated by the circumstances of the times in
> which we live. Our world is full of contradictions and challenges,

but it remains God's creation. The world is wounded by evil, but God loves it still. It is his field in which the sowing of the Word can be renewed so that it would bear fruit once more.

There is no room for pessimism in the minds and hearts of those who know that their Lord has conquered death and that his Spirit works with might in history. We approach this world with humility, but also with determination. This comes from the certainty that the truth triumphs in the end. We choose to see in the world God's invitation to witness to his Name. Our Church is alive and faces the challenges that history brings with the courage of faith and the testimony of her many daughters and sons.

We know that we must face in this world a difficult struggle against the "principalities" and "powers," "the evil spirits" (Ephesians 6:12). We do not ignore the problems that such challenges bring, but they do not frighten us. (Final Message 6)

This sounds a lot like Paul to me. These words are reminiscent of the courage with which Paul faced his own ministerial challenges. Daunted but not defeated! (See 2 Cor 4:7-11.) This is not a naive approach to the mission of the new evangelization. It takes into account the real challenges that exist. As there has always been, so there will be resistance to the message of Jesus Christ. Yet this cannot stop the church from moving forward.

Already in the preparatory document (*Lineamenta*) to the synod, Paul was recalled as an image to keep in mind, especially with regard to the challenges of the mission and the need to rely on the Holy Spirit:

St. Paul the Apostle acknowledges the primary role of the action of the Spirit at a particularly intense and meaningful time for the nascent Church. In fact, some believers felt that other roads were to be taken; others among the first Christians displayed an uncertainty in facing and making some basic choices. The process of evangelization became a process of discernment. Proclamation first requires moments of listening, understanding and interpretation.

In many ways, our times are similar to those in which St. Paul lived. As Christians, we too find ourselves immersed in a period of significant historical and cultural change which we will have greater opportunity to treat later in these pages. Evangelical activity demands that we undertake a similar, corresponding and timely activity of discernment. (Lin 3)

The same document twice cites Paul's cry of "woe" if he does not proclaim the Gospel (Lin 2 and 24) and recalls Paul several times as an example from the church's early history that can provide direction for the future.

The point, of course, is simply this. If the new evangelization is not just a revved up version of the first evangelization, we can nonetheless learn from the apostle Paul and the experience in his churches. Evangelizing is both essential and hard work. It will challenge us to our very foundations, and it may lead down paths that seem at first like dead ends. We may be rejected or mocked. Experience shows in our day that the church's ethical teachings, for example, are sometimes resisted strongly in modern contexts. (Think of questions about marriage, religious liberty, abortion, immigrant protection, the death penalty, secularism, capitalism, the arms race, etc.) But with faith, with confidence in the Holy Spirit, with endurance, and with courage, we can put this vision into action and accomplish the mission given to us in our day. I believe Paul provides a good companion for this journey.

Review and Reflection Questions

1. Why is evangelization such an essential part of the church's self-identity?

2. Do you see any urgent reasons to proclaim the Gospel in modern times? Do you think Catholics have a good sense of their "mission" in the world?

3. What aspects of Paul's evangelical ministry are attractive to you? What aspects do you find troubling or difficult?

4. In what ways would you say you are an "apostle" today?

6

Evangelization Internally and Externally

I have said in chapter 2 that one of the characteristics of the new evangelization is that it is both internally (*ad intra*) and externally (*ad extra*) oriented. The external orientation is evident from the previous chapter. The internal orientation may be less apparent. Both are essential. We now need to expand this concept in regard to the task of the new evangelization and what we can learn from Paul.

Internal and External Evangelization

In reality, this orientation has been a part of the church's message for a long time, but it seems to be one that gets overshadowed by other priorities. Already, Vatican Council II had called the church internally to ongoing conversion (*Ad Gentes Divinitus* 5, 11, 12). Then Pope Paul VI picked up on this theme in his encyclical *Evangelii Nuntiandi* (14, 15). These are conveniently brought together in a comment in the *Instrumentum Laboris* of the synod on the new evangelization, in a passage worth citing at length:

> *The Church is an evangelizer, but she begins by being evangelized herself.* She is "the community of believers, the community of

hope lived and communicated, the community of brotherly love, and she needs to listen unceasingly to what she must believe, to her reasons for hoping, to the new commandment of love. She is the People of God immersed in the world and often tempted by idols, and she always needs to hear the proclamation of the 'mighty works of God,' which converted her to the Lord; she always needs to be called together afresh by him and reunited. In brief, this means that she has a constant need of being evangelized if she wishes to retain freshness, vigor and strength in order to proclaim the Gospel." (IL 37)

The words I have highlighted at the beginning of this citation essentially tell the whole story. This is the internally directed (Latin, *ad intra*) message. The church needs to be evangelized! We who are already believers, who have already accepted the cherished faith in Jesus Christ that we so strongly desire to share with others, must be renewed in that faith over and over again. It reminds me of what I was taught as a seminarian preparing to become a priest and thus regularly preaching the Gospel message. Our homiletics teacher often said, "Remember, gentleman, when you preach, you are first preaching to yourself. If you do not keep that in mind, you will never reach those in the congregation to whom you think you are preaching!"

After several weeks of discussion, the synod participants reiterated this same idea in their closing message, under the section titled "Evangelizing ourselves and opening ourselves to conversion":

We, however, should never think that the new evangelization does not concern us personally. In these days voices among the Bishops were raised to recall that the Church must first of all heed the Word before she could evangelize the world. The invitation to evangelize becomes a call to conversion. (Final Message 5)

This vision for interior renewal in the church, essentially a call to ongoing conversion, was not put forward naively. Several bishops who intervened in the synod admitted that one of the roadblocks to effective evangelization in the past had been the errors that had been made, and especially the arrogance with which the Gospel message had been proclaimed. Thus, they called for conversion *within* the church.

In this regard, the same section of the synod's Final Message admits the challenge that this internal evangelization poses. If the members of the church do not heed this message, we will not be effective in disseminating it among others. People will look at us and say, "See! They can't even live the message, so why should we?" One of the most serious stumbling blocks to evangelization *ad gentes*, to the world at large or externally (Latin, *ad extra*), is the inability of so many of us inside the church to live the Gospel message ourselves.

The synod participants obviously recognized this challenge. In response, however, they called for renewed efforts at internal evangelization and at the same time pointed out that God's grace alone can assure success:

> With humility we must recognize that the poverty and weaknesses of Jesus' disciples, especially of his ministers, weigh on the credibility of the mission. We are certainly aware—we Bishops first of all—that we could never really be equal to the Lord's calling and mandate to proclaim his Gospel to the nations. . . . If this renewal were up to us, there would be serious reasons to doubt. But conversion in the Church, just like evangelization, does not come about primarily through us poor mortals, but rather through the Spirit of the Lord. (Final Message 5)

It is interesting to note that this text points to Jesus' disciples themselves as examples of individuals who had received the call but who also needed to pay attention to their "weaknesses" in order to improve their effectiveness in ministry. One needs to think only of Peter, Judas, and the abandonment of Jesus by the rest of the Twelve in his most needy hour to realize that they were men always in need of renewal!

Little wonder, then, that two final propositions from the synod point out the need for the church's own interior conversion in order to make the new evangelization work. Proposition 22, for instance, says, "Many bishops spoke of the need for renewal in holiness in their own lives, if they are to be true and effective agents of the new evangelization." And the following proposition (23) calls on all church members to heed their own call to personal holiness, in order to present better models to the world for evangelization.

I might emphasize, at this point, that we should make a distinction between the church as "holy"—one of her essential characteristics as founded by Christ—and the weaknesses, sinfulness, and failures of her members. The point is not that we must be absolutely flawless, perfect "saints" in order to preach the message of the Gospel in the world. If we waited for that day, we would never have an outwardly oriented mission.

The point, rather, is that we must do better than we have been doing. The new evangelization, at least at its beginning, was primarily oriented toward Europe, the traditional bastion of Catholic faith. Recent decades have shown the serious decline in the practice of the faith, even in areas like France, Spain, Ireland, Belgium, or Italy, where Catholic identity was part of the fabric of cultural life. The church's image has definitely been tarnished, most visibly through sexual abuse scandals, financial improprieties, and petty squabbling. This makes us more vulnerable to critiques from those outside the church. The new evangelization calls for a reawakening of faith inside, precisely so that we can be better equipped to spread the Gospel message outside.

A Pauline Perspective

Here is where Paul can also be of help. His letters show considerable evidence of a dual orientation, inward and outward, with regard to the Christian task of evangelization. Let us first look at the external orientation.

External Orientation

The most obvious observation about Paul, as I already indicated in the introduction, is that he was an evangelizer *ad gentes* of the highest degree. From the moment of his call, the revelation of Jesus Christ on the road to Damascus, Paul's ministry was outwardly directed to the Gentile world. His identity as an apostle was bound up with this special mission. He was called and sent, Jew though he was, to bring the message of salvation in Jesus Christ to the Gentile world, which is to say the rest of the world. The fact that his mission was also approved by the church's "pillars," or well-established authorities, gave encouragement as well as legitimation to his ministry. Paul never wavered in this external commitment. In fact, he always affirmed it as his divine call, his special mission in the world as an apostle.

Two small examples of this external orientation are quite striking in Paul. The first is the fact that he willingly embraced a mission to cross from Asia, his home area, into Europe, as the result of a "vision" he had (Acts 16:9-10). The story goes thus:

> During the night Paul had a vision: there stood a man of Macedonia pleading with him and saying, "Come over to Macedonia and help us." When he had seen the vision, we immediately tried to cross over to Macedonia, being convinced that God had called us to proclaim the good news to them. We set sail from Troas . . . (Acts 16:9-11a)

We might be tempted to minimize the importance of this move, but that would be a mistake. Even today, when one travels, say, from Greece to Turkey, or vice versa, one notices a considerable cultural change. Greece is European, Turkey is Asian. In Paul's day, this difference was even more striking, despite the fact that the entire area came under the rule of the Roman Empire. For Paul to accept this call was a dramatic move. It meant reaching out to another continent, a different world from his own, in order to carry forth the Gospel message.

The rest, as the saying goes, is history. Paul evangelized throughout Greece, establishing important churches, such as at Philippi, Thessalonica, and Corinth, and ultimately visiting important cities like Athens, where he boldly preached in a foreign context. For Paul, there was no choice. He saw this as the divinely directed mission to which he had been called by the risen Lord Jesus himself.

A second example comes from the late period of Paul's life. When writing to the Romans, a church he had not founded but that he earnestly wanted to visit, he expressed to them his intention to go even farther. He told the Romans that his stay was to be a kind of stepping-stone for a mission to Spain (Rom 15:24, 29), which at that point was one of the farthest outposts in the Roman Empire. This is tantamount to going to the edge of the world, all for the sake of announcing the good news of Jesus Christ.

In other words, these two small examples, as well as the entire witness of Paul's life after his call on the road to Damascus, were oriented outwardly toward the Gentile mission.

Internal Orientation
There is, however, another facet of Paul's ministry that shows he was equally conscious of the need for an *internal* outreach in terms of evangelization. We will look at several indicators.

The first indicator, I suggest, is the fact that Paul, in addition to being a missionary and evangelizer, was a letter writer. Letters were, and are, a means of communication, a way of staying in touch. In Paul's day, letter writing was very important because letters were a substitute presence. Today, perhaps, we are in danger of losing the art of letter writing. Alas, emails, tweets, and text messages are not the same quality of communication. But for Paul, writing letters, and receiving them as well, was a way of keeping in touch with communities that he had founded and that he loved. This was a way to keep in touch with those already within the fold. But we can go deeper into this reality by asking about the content of Paul's letters.

This leads us to the second feature of Paul's internal orientation. If you read through the letters of Paul, you will see a constant thread in them of ethical teaching. This is a subtle indicator of Paul's internal focus, his desire to continue calling his communities to interior renewal or ongoing conversion. Scholars say, in fact, that a significant portion of Paul's letters is devoted to ethical instruction, whether exhortation to do or avoid certain actions, or commendation and affirmation for achievements. Let us examine a few sample passages.

The Corinthian correspondence (1–2 Corinthians) is particularly filled with ethical instruction. Paul recalls for the Corinthians his relationship to them and therefore his right to instruct them in the faith: "If I am not an apostle to others, at least I am to you; for you are the seal of my apostleship in the Lord" (1 Cor 9:2). His apostolic credential, sealed in the existence of the Corinthian community itself, is an important reason he can write to them at length about matters that were of concern to them (1 Cor 1:11; 7:1), as well as issues that he wanted to recall for them (e.g., 1 Cor 11:18-32). Thus, First Corinthians is filled with lengthy advice on ethical matters, such as incest, marriage, divorce and celibacy, proper liturgical celebrations, charisms, and so on.

Furthermore, Paul is aware that sometimes even leaders in the church can be deceiving and thus dangerous to the faith. He warns the Corinthians to be on guard against "false apostles, deceitful workers, disguising themselves as apostles of Christ" (2 Cor 11:13). This is another way of admitting that even church leaders can be bad examples of living the faith one has received in Jesus Christ. Paul tries his best to both warn and exhort, to encourage and bolster the faith he disseminated in such communities. Near the end of many of his letters, he often concludes with final exhortations, such as one we find in Second Corinthians:

> Examine yourselves to see whether you are living in the faith. Test yourselves. Do you not realize that Jesus Christ is in you?—unless, indeed, you fail to meet the test! I hope you will find out that we have not failed. But we pray to God that you may not do anything wrong—not that we may appear to have met the test, but that you may do what is right, though we may seem to have failed. For we cannot do anything against the truth, but only for the truth. For we rejoice when we are weak and you are strong. This is what we pray for, that you may become perfect. (2 Cor 13:5-9)

This is a bold exhortation, one that implicitly recognizes the possibility of the Corinthians not living up to the high standards of the faith, but that also exhorts them to stand firm in that faith.

Why would Paul include such ethical sections directed to his communities if he believed his initial evangelization had been effective? Paul knew that backsliding was always a possibility in his communities. Though he regularly addressed them as "saints" (or the "holy ones"; 1 Cor 1:2; Phil 1:1, etc.), Paul was not naive. He knew that his communities were not perfect images of heaven on earth. They were communities of human beings. Evangelization always required further instruction, further bolstering, ongoing reminders to stay the course or remain faithful. As in the case of the Galatians, Paul often had to warn against backsliding, or reverting (or being seduced) to earlier inappropriate behavior (Gal 1:6-7; 4:19-20). Becoming a follower of Jesus did not always mean one stayed that way in every instance. Thus internally directed messages were always necessary.

Paul's internal instruction, however, was not limited only to communities he founded. When writing to the Romans, for example, he indicates another reason for his visit other than making a temporary stop on his way to Spain. He writes to them in advance:

> For I am longing to see you so that I may share with you some spiritual gift to strengthen you—or rather so that we may be mutually encouraged by each other's faith, both yours and mine. I want you to know, brothers and sisters, that I have often intended

> to come to you (but thus far have been prevented), in order that
> I may reap some harvest among you as I have among the rest of
> the Gentiles. (Rom 1:11-13)

Keeping in mind that the Roman Christian community was already a well-established group of faithful in Paul's day, and that Paul had already become acquainted with a number of them (Rom 16), Paul's appeal here is quite striking. It is a mutual desire for building up the faith. Paul wants to encourage them in their faith, share his own perspective, but also reap some benefit himself as he continues his outward mission. Later ethical sections of the letter show Paul's ongoing outreach to this community. He shares his own perspective of the faith with the Romans so that they, too, may be edified and strengthened.

To conclude this chapter on internal and external evangelization, I offer one more image from Paul with regard to his ceaseless efforts to preach and teach to his communities even after he had moved on to other mission fields. He often contrasted the ethical choices that they faced in the context of their daily lives. The fact is that cultural influences in Paul's day were just as tempting as they are today. There was always the possibility that, without vigilance, the faithful "saints" would turn quickly to deeds unworthy of the name "Christian." We can all too easily be seduced by cultural values contrary to the Gospel message. The letter to the Ephesians expresses this contrast well with an image appropriate to Paul in his conception that "in Christ" we become new creations. He strongly reminds the Ephesians:

> You were taught to put away your former way of life, your old
> self, corrupt and deluded by its lusts, and to be renewed in the
> spirit of your minds, and to clothe yourselves with the new self,
> created according to the likeness of God in true righteousness
> and holiness. (Eph 4:22-24)

The new evangelization faces the same challenge in our day, though the cultural contexts have become ever more complex, and the ethical choices ever more blurry. That is why an internal outreach (to use a paradoxical expression) is as essential as maintaining our commitment to extend the Gospel message to every corner of the globe externally. Both are needed in the new evangelization, and Paul, again, provides a good example of how to maintain the balance.

Review and Reflection Questions

1. In what ways is the new evangelization directed outwardly? In what ways is it directed inwardly?

2. What do you think are the realities in the church today that can impede effective evangelization?

3. How possible is it for the church and its members to accept the message of ongoing conversion and self-evangelization in our day? Do you personally find it easy to accept this message in your own life?

4. What are the main ethical challenges of our day? How well do you think the church confronts these challenges?

Chapter

7

Evangelization as a Universal Responsibility

Many Christians may be tempted to think that the task or mission of evangelization is intended for specialists. We are used to recognizing the particular contribution of missionaries, for instance, in the history of the church. As I explained in chapter 2, however, an aspect of the new evangelization is that it is a universal responsibility. All are called to participate in this mission.

We begin by recalling some specific passages from the synod's documentation. Already the *Instrumentum Laboris* had said in explicit terms:

> Announcing and proclaiming is not the task of any one person or a select few, but rather a gift given to every person who answers the call to faith. Transmitting the faith is not the work of one individual only, but instead, is the responsibility of every Christian and the whole Church, who in this very activity continually rediscovers her identity as a People gathered together by the Spirit to live Christ's presence among us and discover the true face of God, who is Father. (IL 92; also see IL 105)

No one gets off the hook in this ministry. By virtue of our baptism, we are all called into the circle of a people who are committed to spread the message of the Gospel of Jesus Christ far and wide. "The transmission of the faith involves the whole Church" (IL 105).

The same document goes on to connect this mission of evangelization rooted in our baptism with the "priestly" and "prophetic" office of Jesus Christ in which all Christians share by virtue of baptism:

> All the faithful, in virtue of their participation in the common priesthood and the prophetic office of Christ, have an important role in this task of the Church. The lay faithful, in particular, are called upon to show how the Christian faith is a valid response to the pressing problems of life in every age and culture. (IL 118)

It may be useful to recall the source of this imagery. In the Old Testament, the three principal leaders of the people were historically the prophets, priests, and kings. When the early church reflected on Jesus' own ministry, they understandably gravitated to images with which they were familiar. Thus, they invoked these three main models of leadership to explain the "high priesthood" of Jesus Christ. Jesus, the eternal High Priest, is a doctrine found only in the Letter to the Hebrews (Heb 5:1-10; 7:1-3). In reflecting on this powerful image, which itself came from the Old Testament, early Christians came to understand Christ's ministry in a threefold manner. Christ was anointed "prophet" (one who speaks God's Word), "priest" (one who presides over sacrifices made to God), and "king" (one who shepherds the flock, protects them, and governs them).

Subsequently these three titles became associated with the new identity each Christian receives in baptism. It was also later applied more specifically to the ministerial priesthood, so that the church also teaches that ordained priests are configured in a special sacramental way to Christ as prophet, priest, and king. The prior "configuration" to Christ, however, is already made in baptism, whereby one comes to participate in the "priesthood of the faithful" (see 1 Pet 2:9). All the baptized, whether ordained or lay, share this common identity.

I wonder how many Christians realize this fact. It seems to me that, with regard to evangelization, there is an easy temptation to "let others do it." Many Christians, let alone Catholics, do not give second thought to their own mission in the world as people who have been configured to Christ himself and consequently are called to proclaim the good news of the Gospel. All of us are expected to bear witness to Christ in our lives. One of the final propositions of the synod drew attention to this topic by recalling the need for all baptized people to participate in the new evangelization and also be strengthened in their own faith:

> This faith cannot be transmitted in a life which is not modeled after the Gospel or a life which does not find its meaning, truth and future based on the Gospel. For this reason, the New Evangelization for the transmission of the Christian faith calls all believers to renew their faith and their personal encounter with Jesus in the Church, to deepen their appreciation of the truth of the faith and joyfully to share it. (Prop. 7; see also Final Message 8)

Deepening our own commitment to the Lord, then, strengthens us in our desire to share joyfully (not grudgingly!) what we have received in faith with others.

Saint Paul and the Universal Task

Relating Saint Paul to this universal task of the new evangelization is actually rather easy. The *Instrumentum Laboris*, in particular, uses various quotations from the letters of Paul to describe this ministry. Since it is so concisely said, I will quote most of the passage word for word:

> Every person has the right to hear the Gospel of God to humanity, which is Jesus Christ. . . . This right of every person to hear the Gospel is clearly stated by St. Paul. Tireless in his preaching, he looks upon his work of proclaiming the Gospel as a duty, because he understood its universal significance: "For if I preach the Gospel, that gives me no ground for boasting. For necessity is laid upon me. Woe to me if I preach not the Gospel" (1 Cor 9:16). Every man and woman should be able to say, like him, that "Christ loved us and gave himself up for us" (Eph 5:2). Furthermore, every man and woman should be able to feel drawn into an intimate and transforming relationship which the proclamation of the Gospel creates between us and Christ: "It is no longer I who live, but Christ who lives in me; and the life I now live in the flesh I live by faith in the Son of God, who loved me

and gave himself for me" (Gal 2:20). To give others the possibility of having a similar experience requires that someone be sent to proclaim it: "How are men to call upon him in whom they have not believed? And how are they to believe in him of whom they have never heard? And how are they to hear without a preacher?" (Rom 10:14 which repeats Is 52:1). (IL 33)

Two observations are noteworthy about this passage. First, note that it is framed in terms of the explicit "right" of every person to receive the Gospel message and the implicit duty to evangelize. In other words, no one should impede the process of evangelization, since the message of salvation in Jesus Christ is intended for everyone, for the whole world. Nor should one flee the responsibility to share what we ourselves have come to experience. As so often in life, this right also involves an obligation.

The second observation concerns the four Pauline passages cited in the text. Note that the two outer ones (from 1 Corinthians and Romans, respectively) express aspects of the process of evangelization, while the two middle ones (from Ephesians and Galatians, respectively) express the dual reality of the communal and individual aspects of salvation that we experience (that is, the alternation of "us" and "me"). We can thus say once more that the gift we have received in Jesus Christ demands that we share it. Jesus has come to us so that we can go forth to others. This is exactly the point Paul makes in Romans 10 (cited in the text above), when he draws attention to the process of evangelization as a continuum of hearing, believing, and proclaiming.

To these observations on Paul in relation to the universal mission of the new evangelization, I think we can add three more points.

The first additional comment concerns Paul's global view of the human situation. In his most articulate and well-developed letter, Romans, Paul says that all humanity falls under the same specter of sinfulness, so that all humanity consequently needs to be saved (Rom 3:9-26). Paul's argument is very complex, and we cannot delve into it in detail here. But the essential message is summarized in four short verses of that section of Romans:

> For there is no distinction, since all have sinned and fall short of the glory of God; they are now justified by his grace as a gift, through the redemption that is in Christ Jesus, whom God put

forward as a sacrifice of atonement by his blood, effective through
faith. (Rom 3:22b-25)

The message is simple. We are all in the same boat together. All have
sinned, whether Jew or Gentile, and all are in need of God's salvation,
which has been effected through Christ. The universal nature of sinfulness demands the universal salvation in Christ.

Paul, however, goes even further, I think, in his conception of this
universal overview by means of a second reflection. If we return to the
"body of Christ" image that Paul uses to describe the church in its essential identity, we recall that Paul wrote at length about the diversity of
gifts that come from the Holy Spirit and the fact that they are to be used
for building up the body of Christ, the church (1 Cor 12:1-31). We see
once more that no one "gets off the hook." However we are attached to
the body (hand, foot, nose, etc.), we have a role to play. The effectiveness
and health of the body is dependent upon the participation of every part
working together.

Recall Paul's eloquent observation about the body of Christ: "If one
member suffers, all suffer together with it; if one member is honored, all
rejoice together with it" (1 Cor 12:26). I suggest these words can also apply
to the obligation to participate in the building up of the body of Christ.
Paul says that the individual parts of the body cannot simply announce
that they don't belong to the body. Nor can one or another part simply say,
"we don't need you" to other parts (see 1 Cor 12:21). We belong together.
We function together. We rise or fall together.

That is indeed the way the new evangelization should work, at least
ideally. Each member of the church must take up his or her responsibility
and move with it. The new evangelization invites all the members of the
body of Christ to join in the one task that we have all been given in baptism, proclaiming the Lord Jesus by our lives, our words, and our deeds.

Finally, I would add a third comment from Paul on our conduct within
the family of faith we call church. In Galatians, in the context of remarks
about the nature of life in community, Paul reminds the Galatians of the
responsibility they bear by virtue of their membership in the community:

All must test their own work; then that work, rather than their
neighbor's work, will become a cause for pride. For all must carry

their own loads. Those who are taught the word must share in all good things with their teacher. Do not be deceived; God is not mocked, for you reap whatever you sow. If you sow to your own flesh, you will reap corruption from the flesh; but if you sow to the Spirit, you will reap eternal life from the Spirit. So let us not grow weary in doing what is right, for we will reap at harvest time, if we do not give up. So then, whenever we have an opportunity, let us work for the good of all, and especially for those of the family of faith. (Gal 6:4-10)

With these formidable words, Paul seems to be evoking the context of catechetical instruction, whereby one is taught the faith but then is also obligated to share it. We are not supposed to worry about what others are doing but simply examine ourselves. Paul also warns that one day we will be held accountable for our deeds (or lack of them). If these words at first strike us as harsh—"you reap whatever you sow"—Paul does not mean them to be taken that way. He simply is repeating a version of what Jesus himself taught as a way to call his followers to live an upright life. Accountability, or ultimately a final judgment before God, is simply part of the Christian message. Jesus himself taught about accountability and judgment (Matt 5:22; 12:36; 25:31-46; etc.). Paul, using his well-known contrast between the "flesh" and the "Spirit," exhorts the Galatians to accept their responsibilities individually and collectively to one another. We should be working together for the good of all, especially "the family of faith," that is, those who are already believers, members of the church.

These words of Paul, I believe, give us another glimpse of the universal mission to which we are called in the new evangelization. No one is exempted, nor is anyone excluded. All should be engaged for the good of the total group. If each one takes responsibility for his or her actions, the Spirit will assure a good outcome. Paul's confidence in the Holy Spirit never wavered, even in the context of a troublesome community like the Galatians (5:5; 6:1), where some were being tempted to abandon the Gospel message they had received from Paul.

Review and Reflection Questions

1. Why does every Christian have a duty to engage in evangelization?

2. What is meant by "the priesthood of the faithful"? How does it relate to baptism?

3. How well do you understand your responsibilities as a Christian? Do you have any anxieties or fears about your Christian or Catholic identity?

4. Practically, what steps can you take to evangelize or share your faith?

Individual and Communal Dimensions of Faith

Another characteristic of the new evangelization, as we saw in chapter 2, is that it is not only targeted to individuals but to whole cultures. Bolstering such an assertion is the recognition that faith has both individual and communal dimensions, both of which are essential.

Perhaps the clearest statement of the dual dimension, individual and communal, comes from Pope Benedict XVI's *motu proprio* on the Year of Faith:

> A Christian may never think of belief as a private act. Faith is choosing to stand with the Lord so as to live with him. This "standing with him" points towards an understanding of the reasons for believing. Faith, precisely because it is a free act, also demands social responsibility for what one believes. The Church on the day of Pentecost demonstrates with utter clarity this public dimension of believing and proclaiming one's faith fearlessly to every person. . . .
>
> Profession of faith is an act both personal and communitarian. . . . As we read in the *Catechism of the Catholic Church*: " 'I believe' is the faith of the Church professed personally by each believer, principally during baptism. 'We believe' is the faith of the Church confessed by the bishops assembled in council or

more generally by the liturgical assembly of believers." (*Porta
Fidei* 10; *Catechism* 167)

This is clearly a stance of both/and rather than either/or. There are some
Christians who want to maintain that the most important aspect of faith
is only the individual confession. They consequently see no importance to
the "church" as a community of the faithful. In fact, they often rely on Paul
to defend their position. In Romans, Paul says, "if you confess with your
lips that Jesus is Lord and believe in your heart that God raised him from
the dead, you will be saved" (Rom 10:9). This is certainly a true statement,
and one cannot deny the importance of stating one's own faith explicitly
and firmly. *Porta Fidei*, indeed, quotes the next line of this passage: "For
one believes with the heart and so is justified, and one confesses with the
mouth and so is saved" (Rom 10:10). But this perspective is only half the
story. As we shall see, Paul simultaneously recognized communal dimensions of the faith that must also be acknowledged.

The *Instrumentum Laboris* of the synod itself gave due attention to
both aspects of faith:

> The Christian faith is not simply teachings, wise sayings, a code
> of morality or a tradition. The Christian faith is a true encounter
> and relationship with Jesus Christ. Transmitting the faith means
> to create in every place and time the conditions which lead to
> this encounter between the person and Jesus Christ. The goal of
> all evangelization is to create the possibility for this encounter,
> which is, at one and the same time, intimate, personal, public
> and communal. (IL 18)

Faith is both a personal encounter and subsequent testimony. It is a public and communal act, in which the believer places herself or himself in
relationship with others who share the same faith. This same perspective
is reinforced elsewhere in the *Instrumentum Laboris* (24, 26, 33), using
at times passages from Saint Paul to show that faith is both personal and
communal in nature.

This perspective was already found in the *Lineamenta* for the synod: "The
transmission of the faith is never an individual, isolated undertaking, but a
communal, ecclesial event" (Lin 2). Every individual is called to conversion

and to encounter the risen Christ. But this experience of personal faith leads one to join others in transmitting or communicating the faith. Faith involves the appreciation of others, especially in the context of sharing that faith and participating in a communal life through which believers can help one another sustain the initial fervor of faith and make it grow.

The Final Message of the synod picked up on this dual reality with two images, one from the Bible and one from Blessed Pope John XXIII, the pope who startled the Vatican and the world by calling for, and then convening, Vatican Council II.

At the beginning of their Final Message, the synod participants recalled the image of the Samaritan woman at the well, the beautiful story from John's gospel that is used often in the season of Lent (John 4:4-42; Final Message 1). They recall how the woman encountered Jesus personally (as indeed so many individuals do in the Fourth Gospel) at a well, and Jesus offered her "living water."

This image is then applied to modern life. Like this woman, women and men today are also thirsting. We all are seeking that water of life that will truly quench our thirst. The Samaritan woman was at first skeptical but slowly, gradually came to believe in Jesus as the Messiah and then went off and gave witness to others in her village. Her faith led others to faith, for she called them to come and hear Jesus for themselves and they said, "It is no longer because of what you said that we believe, for we have heard for ourselves, and we know that this is truly the Savior of the world" (John 4:42).

If we must in fact embrace faith individually—and surely we have to affirm our faith as individuals in order to live it properly—it does not end there. It spreads forth to others. It leads to a communal dimension. Like a pebble thrown into a pond, its ripple effects go out in every direction and touch the distant shores.

This biblical image, found at the very beginning of the Final Message, is balanced by another one that is closely related to it. As the Samaritan woman encountered Jesus at the well, so Pope John XXIII used to evoke the image of "the village fountain," the place where people would go to quench their thirst but also to encounter others and enter into conversation with them. The Final Message employed this image in this way:

> No one person or group in the Church has exclusive right to the work of evangelization. It is the work of ecclesial communities

as such, where one has access to all the means for encountering Jesus: the Word, the sacraments, fraternal communion, charitable service, mission. In this perspective, the role of the parish emerges above all as the presence of the Church where men and women live, "the village fountain," as John XXIII loved to call it, from which all can drink, finding in it the freshness of the Gospel. (Final Message 8; see also 3)

These interrelated images illustrate the main principle. Faith is both an individual decision, a purposeful acceptance of the gift that has been offered to us by God in his Son Jesus Christ, and a lived response that finds a home in the community of faith, which we call "church." The new evangelization encompasses both these realities.

Learning from Paul

Seeing both individual and communal dimensions of the Christian faith in Saint Paul is not very difficult. Both the *Instrumentum Laboris* and the Final Message of the synod use certain Pauline passages to illustrate this point. But I wish to take the larger picture of Paul to show that Paul can be quite strong on both sides of this equation.

The Individual Dimension

On the individual side, we can cite Paul explicitly, apart from the passage in Romans 10. For example, in Galatians, Paul speaks eloquently of the personal realization that he has been saved by Jesus Christ:

> For through the law I died to the law, so that I might live to God. I have been crucified with Christ; and it is no longer I who live, but it is Christ who lives in me. And the life I now live in the flesh I live by faith in the Son of God, who loved me and gave himself for me. (Gal 2:19-20)

The intimate admission that Jesus Christ loved *me* and died for *me* may be quite surprising, especially for Catholics, who are used to emphasizing the communal nature of salvation. Paul here sounds almost like an Evangelical Christian who is more at home with a "Jesus-and-me" attitude than with anything approximating a church identity. But there it is. It is reinforced as well by the use of the first-person pronoun "I" in terms of his new life he now lives in Christ. Paul clearly emphasizes his personal faith, which in fact is apparent in other ways, such as his insistence in virtually all of his letters of his personal apostolic call by Christ.

Paul brings this personal dimension forth in other instances worth recalling. In Philippians, for instance, Paul speaks forthrightly about how he understands this personal transformation that has come over him in faith:

> I regard everything as loss because of the surpassing value of knowing Christ Jesus my Lord. For his sake I have suffered the loss of all things, and I regard them as rubbish, in order that I may gain Christ and be found in him, not having a righteousness of my own that comes from the law, but one that comes through faith in Christ, the righteousness from God based on faith. I want to know Christ and the power of his resurrection and the sharing of his sufferings by becoming like him in his death, if somehow I may attain the resurrection from the dead. (Phil 3:8-11)

Are these words not striking? Note how frequently Paul again employs the first-person pronoun "I" and also speaks of "Christ Jesus *my* Lord." (See also 1 Tim 1:12-16 and 2 Tim 4:6-8 for more personal testimony on the part of Paul.)

In short, Paul does not shy away from expressing the personal dimension of faith in ways that might make some Catholics squirm a bit. I have sometimes been asked by Catholics, made nervous by rather aggressive Protestant evangelizers who knock on their door and inquire if they have accepted Jesus Christ as their personal Lord and Savior, how to respond to this question. My reply is rather simple: "Well, I hope you said 'yes,' because in fact we Catholics believe the same thing. But we add immediately that the salvation we have experienced personally has another whole dimension that cannot be left out. Yes, Jesus Christ died for *me*, but not just for me alone. He also gave himself for *us*, for all sinful humanity."

The Communal Dimension

Paul always recognized this communal dimension of faith in addition to the personal. Let me propose two examples here.

The first example concerns his use of the expression "body of Christ" to describe the nature of the church. Paul seems to be the first one to use this marvelous image, and he does so in First Corinthians in the context of affirming the Corinthians' individual charisms, given to them by the Holy Spirit, and the true purpose of these precious gifts. He employs the image of the human body, with its diverse parts (ears, eyes, feet, nose, etc.) that must work together for the good of the whole body (1 Cor 11:14-26). So interconnected is the body that Paul says, "If one member suffers, all suffer together with it; if one member is honored, all rejoice together with it" (1 Cor 12:26). He even goes so far as to call to attention the less dignified parts of the body, which are just as essential (or even more so!) as any other part. Paul's punch line for this example is poignant: "Now you [plural] are the body of Christ and individually members of it" (1 Cor 12:27).

While it is true that Paul is using this image in relation to different charisms in the church, similarly one can say that however the gift of faith is manifested in an individual's life, and whatever gift he or she has been given, it is not for the sake of that person alone. It is to contribute to the good of the whole group, to build up the community of faith, to enhance the body of Christ (see 1 Cor 14:12).

Paul even uses himself as an example. He says he had the gift of tongues, the ability to speak in ineffable foreign tongues to the glory of God, which was a prized gift among some of the Corinthians, who seemed to see it as indicating a higher spiritual status. In response, Paul remarks that his gift was even greater than that of all the Corinthians, but "in church I would rather speak five words with my mind, in order to instruct others also, than ten thousand words in a tongue" (1 Cor 14:19). This is tantamount to saying that we must recognize the true goal of the gifts we have each been given in faith. They are for the good of a larger group, the community of faith. In fact, for Paul an important word is "fellowship" or "communion" (Greek, *koinōnia*). Anything that breaks this fellowship apart, or weakens it because of an overemphasis on the individual, moves in the opposite direction of true faith.

This leads us to a second way in which Paul emphasizes the importance of the communal dimension of the faith. His regular practice of including the names of others in the greetings or closings of his letters shows that Paul saw himself in relationship to others who were his colleagues or "coworkers" (e.g., 1 Cor 1:1; 2 Cor 1:1; Gal 1:2). He also addresses his letters to the "church" or "churches" of a particular location, indicating that even his written communications are meant to be shared with the larger community of faith (e.g., Gal 1:2; 1 Thess 1:1). Moreover, although he can invite prayer for himself (Rom 15:30; Eph 6:19), often he speaks in the plural, both promising prayer for his communities and inviting their prayers for him and his colleagues (Rom 1:9; 10:1; 2 Cor 9:14). Most importantly, Paul frequently uses the plural "we" or "us" with regard to the faith that has come through Jesus Christ (Rom 5:8; 8:34; 1 Cor 1:30; 10:6; Gal 3:13; 1 Thess 5:10; etc.).

If God has called us individually by name, and if we have been baptized into Christ Jesus who has given us the great gift of faith, it is primarily for the purpose of building up the human community. For Paul, as well as for the new evangelization, the individual and communal aspects of the faith must be respected equally. Baptism bestows on us individually a new identity, but it is not merely for our own good. We are thereby brought into a community of faith that celebrates together, prays together, works together as the one, indivisible body of Christ.

The Cultural Aspect

To bring this theme to a close, I must add a final comment about culture. The new evangelization has emphasized that "whole cultures" are to be evangelized, and not just individuals. The complex modern reality of cultures surely makes this a daunting task. How does one exactly bring a whole culture into contact with the faith?

Throughout church history, missionaries have always endeavored to accomplish this very task. This is just as urgent a task in our day because cultural influences are extremely powerful. The *Instrumentum Laboris* underlines this fact at several points, but most especially when evoking the influence of secularization and antireligious sentiment that has become characteristic of many modern cultures (IL 52–62). The same document, however, notes that there can be positive influences from cultures too (IL 54). Evangelizers cannot simply set themselves as opposed to everything in a local culture if they desire to be heard and received.

I see culture as a two-way street. Cultural influences are indeed very communal. We all live under peer pressure or a desire to be like our neighbors, especially when it comes to success in worldly terms. I also suggest, however, that Paul understood well the impact of cultures. He, an Asian, had to deal with the realities of a kind of "European" mindset such as was evident in the multicultural, pluralistic setting of Athens or Rome. He, a Jew, albeit one who had become a follower of Jesus Christ, had to live in an incredibly diverse and multilingual environment such as existed in the ancient Mediterranean basin of his day. Acts, in particular, portrays Paul as willing to confront these realities and adapt to them. He was even willing to use his "trump card" of Roman citizenship to appeal to the emperor when his life was ultimately threatened (Acts 22:27-28; 25:11-12).

I believe Paul provides a good model of trying to work with, while not being seduced by, the cultures in which we now find ourselves. Paul was the first to encourage his communities to reject the secular and anti-religious values of his day (Gal 5:19-21), but he also knew when to adapt so as not to lead others into distress (1 Cor 8:13). Somewhere there is a middle ground the church will need to find for the new evangelization to be effective. We need solid, faith-filled individuals, but we also need stalwart communities who support one another and are stable enough not simply to cave in to outside cultural pressures when the message we offer is rejected or ignored. We also need wise leaders who know how to understand modern cultures in order to accept what is good or positive in them, and to reject what is bad or negative.

Review and Reflection Questions

1. Why does faith always involve both individual and communal dimensions? Describe ways in which both are present in your own life.

2. To what degree do you experience a good sense of "community" in your church or parish? Are there ways the communal dimension could be strengthened?

3. What are the main cultural challenges facing the church today? What positive values do you see in them? What negative values?

4. How does Paul serve as a good model for a balance between individual and communal dimensions of the faith? Do you think Paul was realistic in this regard?

Chapter

9

Sustaining the Mission:
Prayer, Word, Sacrament,
Justice and Peace, and Ethics

Throughout the synod on the new evangelization, the participating bishops often reflected on the ways in which this special and urgent mission of the church could be sustained in the face of the many challenges that exist in our day. Unsurprisingly, they found comfort in many of the traditional spiritual practices of the church. We will focus on five of them that stand out.

The Final Message of the synod stated the following as an overarching perspective on the importance of the encounter with Christ:

> The Church is the space offered by Christ in history where we can encounter him, because he entrusted to her his Word, the Baptism that makes us God's children, his Body and his Blood, the grace of forgiveness of sins above all in the sacrament of Reconciliation, the experience of communion that reflects the very mystery of the Holy Trinity, the strength of the Spirit that generates charity towards all. (Final Message 3)

Many of the basic elements of the church's life are seen here. The church is the privileged place where one encounters the risen Christ. It is a community of prayer that reflects on and proclaims the Word of God, celebrates the sacraments, works for justice and peace, and is always aware of the need for putting into action the ethical demands of the Gospel. Let's take a closer look at each of these.

Prayer

In the Final Message alone, prayer is mentioned some twelve times throughout the document. In particular, especially during the Year of Faith, importance was given to educating the young in prayer and promoting prayer and other spiritual practices among families (Final Message 7, 13; also Prop. 36). Christians are always people of prayer. In silence we encounter God, and from our hearts we respond to God with our own words, whether of praise, thanksgiving, or petition.

Paul's letters, too, exhibit an incredibly broad understanding of prayer. Paul was a man of prayer who led his communities in prayer, prayed for them, and willingly asked for their prayers for him and his companions. Paul also gave us the advice to "pray always" (1 Thess 5:17), that is, in all circumstances to invoke the Lord's name. Paul's letters contain many examples of prayers, whether thanksgiving, praise, or petition (e.g., 2 Cor 9:14; Phil 1:3-5; Eph 3:14-21; Rom 11:33-36), and we can easily read them and use them as our own prayers today.

Sometimes, of course, we run into dry periods of prayer. We occasionally don't know how to pray or what to say. At such moments, we need to remember that simply being conscious of God and being in God's presence, even in silence, is the most important value. Prayer is not only about speaking to God but *listening* for God. Nonetheless, Paul reminded the Romans that even when we are at a loss for prayer, the Holy Spirit comes to our aid and provides just the right expression. As Paul puts it, "Likewise the Spirit helps us in our weakness; for we do not know how to pray as we ought, but that very Spirit intercedes with sighs too deep for words" (Rom 8:26).

Paul's point seems to be behind the statement in Proposition 36 from the synod on the "spiritual dimension of the new evangelization," which says, "The principal agent of evangelization is the Holy Spirit, who opens hearts and converts them to God." Ultimately, the new evangelization, as all activities in the church, must be firmly grounded in a solid prayer life if we want it to flourish. We surrender to the Holy Spirit, and we consciously engage our minds and hearts in prayer to God who has called us into being.

Word

Another spiritual aspect that is central to the new evangelization is serious reflection on the Sacred Scriptures as the Word of God. This point, in fact, had already been highlighted in Pope Benedict XVI's apostolic exhortation *Verbum Domini*, the result of the previous synod. This document calls for appreciating the Scriptures as God's holy Word more deeply. Three of its teachings are especially pertinent for our purposes here. First, both study and prayer of the Word of God are essential to exploring the Scriptures properly. Historical and theological or spiritual dimensions of the text go hand in hand (*Verbum Domini* 35). Thus, there is a place for real study of Scripture formally as well as for using it for personal spiritual enrichment.

Second, the pope emphasizes the privileged place of Scripture in the church's liturgy (*Verbum Domini* 52, 54–55). (In fact, the document's title—*Verbum Domini* or The Word of the Lord—alludes to the proclamation of Scripture at Mass, to which we respond, *Deo gratias* or "Thanks be to God.") Consequently, all are encouraged to prepare to hear the Word proclaimed at Mass and other liturgical celebrations with care. Preachers (bishops, priests, deacons) need to prepare good scripturally based homilies, and laypeople, readers or lectors especially, need to reflect on the readings in advance to receive the divine message better.

Finally, the document highlights the rediscovery of the ancient practice of *lectio divina* (holy reading), from which all Christians can gain deeper insight into Scripture. This practice of meditating on Scripture is regaining popularity today, as many Christians rediscover the value of reading and prayerfully reflecting on the Bible regularly. Protestants and other Christians have also expressed appreciation for this development.

This basic orientation on the Word of God is picked up in the Final Message (4) and propositions (11) from the synod on the new evangelization, just as it was underlined in the preparatory and working documents (such as Lin 13; IL 19, 22). Sacred Scripture is one of the privileged places where we can encounter the risen Lord. In his sacred, inspired Word, we meet him once more speaking to us in our own day.

Turning back to Paul, we also see the importance of the Word of God, understood in his day as primarily the Old Testament. Paul's letters are filled both with quotations from and allusions to many passages from the Old Testament. He apparently memorized large parts of the Scriptures, but he may also have used a handbook of key passages with which he traveled. (Keep in mind that in Paul's day the Scriptures existed in scrolls, not convenient books, so he would not have had his own personal Bible. Besides, reading and writing were specialized skills, limited mostly to scribes, though Paul was well educated and could do both.) In any case, Paul reflected at length and deeply on the message found in Scripture. He used them to bolster his own teachings and to demonstrate how Jesus Christ was the fulfillment of Israel's holy writings, especially the prophets (Rom 16:26).

Two specific examples can illustrate Paul's deep appreciation of Scripture. In Romans, Paul says,

> For whatever was written in former days was written for our instruction, so that by steadfastness and by the encouragement of the scriptures we might have hope. (Rom 15:4)

Here he clearly indicates that the ancient Scriptures are for our benefit. They are not merely ancient words. Paul understood Scripture as divine communication that could be understood and applied anew in different circumstances.

Another Pauline passage underlines the usefulness of the Scriptures for all believers:

> All scripture is inspired by God and is useful for teaching, for reproof, for correction, and for training in righteousness, so that everyone who belongs to God may be proficient, equipped for every good work. (2 Tim 3:16-17)

In other words, the Scriptures can be used well for our benefit, to give us direction in life and to call us back to the right path when we wander off it.

These are merely two examples from Paul's letters that show the importance of reading, reflecting on, and using the Sacred Scriptures, which communicate God's will for us in our day, much as they did for our ancestors in the faith. Of course, for us now, Paul's letters themselves, as well as the rest of the New Testament, constitute "the Word of God." We might say that his proclamation of the Word has borne fruit by multiplying the Word itself. His letters are now part of that great tradition.

Sacrament

A third element to sustain the new evangelization concerns the celebration of the sacraments. The documents on the new evangelization all give emphasis to the sacramental life of the church, especially the Eucharist, which Vatican II called "the source and summit" of our faith (*Lumen Gentium* 11). All seven sacraments, however, are intimately related to the Word of God and constitute sources of grace—spiritual energy, we might say—for the life of all Christians. Naturally, the new evangelization gives a certain emphasis to baptism, confirmation, Eucharist, and reconciliation, the four sacraments that most readily touch every Catholic's life. The first three are uniquely identified as the "sacraments of initiation" (Lin 18; IL 134; see also *Catechism* 1212), by which every Christian enters the new life of Christ and is joined to the community of disciples. (The *Instrumentum Laboris* [136] notes that there is no uniformity of practice in the church on administering the sacrament of confirmation, but it is essentially the sacrament of "sealing" our faith or taking adult responsibility for it.)

As for reconciliation, it is obviously a sacrament for all people who, when we recognize our sinfulness and human failings, come to God with a sincere desire to be forgiven and given a new start in life. Many dioceses have established the practice, especially during the season of Lent, of inviting people back to the church through this sacrament. There is always hope through reconciliation, no matter how seriously we have sinned or violated God's commandments.

In addition to the four fundamental sacraments, the church accepts three others that relate to specific circumstances: holy orders (for those with a vocation to ordained ministry), matrimony (for those with a vocation to the married life), and anointing of the sick (for those who are seriously ill or in danger of death). These are mentioned in passing in the documents on the new evangelization. Particular emphasis is given to promoting vocations to the priesthood and religious life.

Why are the sacraments important? Taking its cue from the *Catechism*, the *Instrumentum Laboris* explains why the sacraments are so essential to the faith:

> Thus, starting from the fundamental elements taken from Sacred
> Scripture, ecclesial tradition has created a pedagogy for transmit-
> ting the faith, which is developed according to the four major
> divisions of the Roman *Catechism*: the Creed, the sacraments,
> the commandments and the Lord's Prayer. (IL 100)

The sacraments are part of a larger "pedagogy," a way of communicating and strengthening the faith among the community of believers. The
sacraments communicate God's grace, call the church to faithful witness,
and sustain the faith. Along with the Creed, the Ten Commandments,
and the Lord's Prayer (the Our Father), the sacraments are a crucial part
of the ordinary life of all Christians.

Although the form of the sacraments developed over a long period
of time, we see already in the letters of Paul the essential nature of the
sacraments for Christian life. Paul's letters show evidence of at least the
sacraments of baptism, Eucharist, reconciliation, and holy orders.

Paul himself was baptized (Acts 9:18), and baptism obviously was
part of the early church's evangelization efforts, though the practice was
not always uniform (see Acts 8:13, 38; 10:47-48). His understanding of
baptism, while not described in detail, was profound. Baptism is nothing
less than putting on Christ, being baptized into his death, so that we can
experience also the resurrection (Rom 6:3; Gal 3:27; also see Col 2:12).
At Corinth, Paul had to address the issue of baptism directly when it
became associated with supporting one or another faction in the community. Some in the community were apparently following certain leaders
who had baptized them, resulting in the creation of different "parties" or
factions in Corinth. Paul sternly warned the Corinthians to cease their
divisions. He insisted that baptism was never his primary mission as an
apostle (1 Cor 1:17)—evangelization was. Yet he acknowledged that he
administered baptism, and his letters indicate that it was a foundational
sacrament of initiation into the Christian faith.

As regards the other sacraments, Paul also underscored the importance of celebrating the Eucharist with proper respect (1 Cor 11:23-32),
and saw his ministry, in part, as being an "ambassador" for Christ in
the ministry of reconciliation (2 Cor 5:16-21). He also engaged in the
"laying on of hands," the ancient gesture of passing on authority to other
ministers in the church, especially when he himself would head out on

further evangelization efforts (see Acts 13:3; 19:6; also Phil 1:1). This action, along with the invocation of the Holy Spirit, became characteristic of later "ordination" ceremonies by which one enters the "order" of ordained ministers (whether bishop, priest, or deacon). Paul seemingly never left his communities bereft of leadership. Like a good shepherd, he affirmed good leadership in his communities. When he moved on to other pastures, he took care to leave good shepherds behind to tend the flock.

In short, maintaining good sacramental practice was both characteristic of Paul and is an essential feature of the new evangelization.

Justice and Peace

The church has regularly proclaimed its commitment to justice and peace from the very beginning of its existence. Indeed, Jesus himself was obviously committed to justice and peace, though his ministry of proclaiming "the good news" of God's kingdom paradoxically brought violence against him and his followers. The social teachings of the Catholic Church constitute one of the great unsung resources of our tradition, which unfortunately often get overshadowed by high-profile, sensitive, or controversial ethical issues, such as those regarding sexuality or medical ethics. In any case, the documents on the new evangelization called for a renewed commitment to the church's social teaching, and an appeal to work for justice and peace. Just a few examples will suffice to illustrate this point.

In calling for sensitivity to the world's poor and the constant need to be attentive to them, the Final Message of the synod stated,

> The gesture of charity, on the other hand, must also be accompanied by commitment to justice, with an appeal that concerns all, poor and rich. Hence, the social doctrine of the Church is integral to the pathways of the new evangelization, as well as the formation of Christians to dedicate themselves to serve the human community in social and political life. (Final Message 12)

In the context of noting tensions that sometimes exist even in interreligious dialogues, the same document calls for a commitment to peace in the world. Religions, especially, should be instruments of peace and harmony, and not the reason for divisions and violence (Final Message

10; also Prop. 14). A similar point was made in the *Instrumentum Laboris*, which noted the need to promote "justice, freedom, peace and solidarity" even in the context of the diversity that exists in the world's religions (IL 35; also 122 and 130).

With regard to Paul and his churches, there is an underlying vision of the need for justice and peace in the world. Paul's basic vocabulary of God's "righteousness" comes from the same realm as the concept of "justice." God is the source of all righteousness and justice. God alone grants this to all humanity, all of us sinners, who are not really in and of ourselves worthy of the dignity God has bestowed upon us through Jesus Christ. In the context of calling all members of the community to be more socially conscious about one another, Paul writes to the Romans a revealing passage that touches this theme:

> Let us therefore no longer pass judgment on one another, but resolve instead never to put a stumbling block or hindrance in the way of another. . . . For the kingdom of God is not food and drink but righteousness and peace and joy in the Holy Spirit. The one who thus serves Christ is acceptable to God and has human approval. Let us then pursue what makes for peace and for mutual upbuilding. (Rom 14:13, 17-19)

It would be hard to find a more forthright call to justice and peace. I would also add that if this commitment is not found in the community of the faithful itself, it will also be difficult in the new evangelization to proclaim it to outsiders. Paul called the Christian community to account in this regard, and he set the bar rather high.

As regards peace, we need to recall that for Paul, the concept is more than simply the absence of war and violence. Already in his Jewish background, the concept of peace (Hebrew, *shalom*, which is still used as a greeting among Jews) is really a prayerful wish for a deep, interior calm and total well-being. It constitutes the deepest kind of human harmony and inner contentment that only God can bring. Paul regularly invokes "peace" in the openings and closings of his letters. He uses it in conjunction with "grace," for surely these are two of the most precious gifts that come from God (e.g., 1 Cor 1:3; 2 Cor 1:2; 13:11, 13; Gal 1:3; 1 Thess 1:1; 5:23, 28). The letter to the Colossians also exhorts the community to let peace reign among them: "Let the peace of Christ reign in your hearts" (Col 3:15, author's translation).

If the new evangelization efforts are to be effective, the church must continue to stand for justice and peace. Christians should be pristine examples of this commitment in a world where injustice and violence are regular occurrences.

Ethics

It almost goes without saying that much of the message of the new evangelization is a renewed call to all believers to put their faith in action by living an ethically upright life. In a world where corruption, self-advancement, and deception are part of daily life, the Christian commitment to ethics should be self-evident. The message of Jesus is obviously oriented to righteousness, understood as a living out of the commandments of God, especially love of God and neighbor (Mark 12:28-34; Matt 22:34-40).

The documentation on the new evangelization certainly underscores the importance of ethics in Christian living (Lin 20; Prop. 56; IL 62). In particular, the so-called "theological virtues" of faith, hope, and love are given precedence because they are so global in orientation. They are the root of all virtues. Many of the final propositions of the synod drew attention to the need to address the many ethical issues of our day, and to do so within the framework of our Christian faith. We do not try to lead ethically upright lives to gain glory, to advance ourselves, or to impress others. We do it because it is the right thing to do. It is our human response to the divine call of faith. Thus, we as a community of faith are willing to challenge threats to religious freedom, to protect human life from its natural conception to natural death, to defend the poor and the disenfranchised, to protect immigrants and outsiders, to work for interreligious tolerance, and to eradicate violence, hatred, and bigotry.

Paul's letters exhibit no less a firm commitment to this ethical viewpoint. In fact, as mentioned earlier, there are large sections of ethical teaching in Paul that address many specific issues of his day, some of which remain current in our own time (e.g., 1 Cor 7–8; Rom 12:9-21). Moreover, Paul is willing to contrast the two main options that lie before us. He uses the terminology of light/darkness or spirit/flesh to show the choice that lies before people. Galatians provides a good example:

Now the works of the flesh are obvious: fornication, impurity, licentiousness, idolatry, sorcery, enmities, strife, jealousy, anger, quarrels, dissensions, factions, envy, drunkenness, carousing, and things like these. I am warning you, as I warned you before: those who do such things will not inherit the kingdom of God. By contrast, the fruit of the Spirit is love, joy, peace, patience, kindness, generosity, faithfulness, gentleness, and self-control. (Gal 5:19-23; see also 1 Thess 5:4-11)

Paul minces no words. He looks around his contemporary world and sees all kinds of available temptations to be resisted. He also sees the possible "fruit" (note the singular!) of the Spirit. Christians do not see ethical deeds apart from the larger picture of our entire life well-lived. We are called to bear "good fruit" in our lives (see also Matt 12:33; Luke 6:43-45).

This is also why Paul himself spoke so poetically on the priority of love (charity) above all the other virtues (1 Cor 13). In the end, good ethical decisions are based on love, which was also the primary commandment of Jesus of Nazareth (Matt 5:44; Mark 12:33; Luke 6:35; John 13:34). Paul himself knew of this command of Jesus and recalled it for his communities (Rom 12:10; 13:10; Gal 5:14). Saint Augustine once said, "love and do what you will," which was not a blanket call to do anything you want. Rather, it affirms that love is the priority that orients us properly to live an ethically upright life (see *Deus Caritas Est* 34).

In conclusion, these five elements are all essential to the new evangelization. We have obviously not touched every possible dimension, for the documents on the new evangelization are extensive and detailed. We can, however, by focusing on these five concepts, see that Paul has much to teach us in responding to the call of the new evangelization. He would be "at home" in this world in the sense that the task of the new evangelization is similar to, if not exactly the same as, the evangelistic mission in his day. If we can find the strength and courage to respond as he did, we should have every confidence that we can also succeed in proclaiming the good news as he did.

Review and Reflection Questions

1. In what ways is Paul's approach to sustaining evangelization related to the new evangelization?

2. Of the five elements highlighted in this chapter, which one(s) is easiest for you? Which one(s) poses the greatest challenge?

3. What connections do you see between faith and ethics?

4. In your estimation, what are the most burning issues facing the church today in the modern world? How would you encourage fellow Christians to respond to these issues?

Chapter

10

The Urgency of the Mission: Challenges for the New Evangelization

One of the most frequently cited passages from Paul in all the literature associated with the new evangelization is the one we have quoted before: "If I proclaim the gospel, this gives me no ground for boasting, for an obligation is laid on me, and woe to me if I do not proclaim the gospel!" (1 Cor 9:16). Paul sounds a note of urgency here that cannot be overlooked. But why is the new evangelization so urgent? And why have several popes now exhorted the church to awaken to the urgency of this mission?

The reasons are no doubt multiple, but two stand out. First, as both Pope John Paul II and Pope Benedict XVI emphasized during their pontificates, the sad state of affairs regarding fallen-away Catholics, or those who have let the faith recede far into the background of their lives, demands an urgent response. The church would be irresponsible if it simply walked away from this reality. In fact, I think it is important that we ask the question of why people do abandon their faith. Only if we can be realistic in seeking an answer to this question can we strategize ways to reignite their faith. I believe this means honestly confronting weaknesses in our own Catholic approach to evangelization in the course of history.

A second and more fundamental urgency, however, stems from the nature of evangelization itself. When one has been given such a powerful gift as the Christian faith asserts, namely, salvation in Christ Jesus, one cannot hesitate or delay in "announcing the good news"—in a nutshell, evangelizing. One does not keep this gift wrapped up in a box sitting on a shelf. Jesus came to draw people together and to form a new community, no longer based solely on blood lines but on discipleship. Jesus came to form a *family* of faith.

This urgency appears in all the documentation on the new evangelization, already expressed in Vatican II's decree *Ad Gentes Divinitus*, Pope Paul VI's encyclical *Evangelii Nuntiandi*, and the more recent documentation from Pope John Paul II and Pope Benedict XVI, as well as the synod documents. In fact, after the *Lineamenta* was proposed for the synod, the *Instrumentum Laboris* points out the reaction felt in many parts of the globe:

> More than one response reported that simply the announcement
> of the topic and that work had begun on the *Lineamenta* caused
> Christian communities to feel stronger and more committed to
> the urgent character today of the imperative of the new evangeli-
> zation, and, as a further benefit, to enjoy a sense of communion
> which allowed them to approach everyday challenges with a dif-
> ferent spirit. (IL 15)

This urgency was also expressed in the preface with these words:

> The goal of evangelization today is, as always, the transmission
> of the Christian faith. . . .
>   This renewed dynamism in the Christian community will
> lead to renewed missionary activity (*missio ad gentes*), now more
> urgent than ever, given the large number of people who do not
> know Jesus Christ, in not only far-off countries but also those
> already evangelized. (IL preface)

Example of Jesus and the Apostles

This urgency of the mission to transmit the faith honestly and to evangelize wherever we can should not surprise us. The entire New Testament gives more than adequate testimony to the urgency of proclaiming the

Gospel. Jesus himself, once he had been baptized, set off quickly under the guidance of the Holy Spirit to go throughout Galilee and Judea preaching, teaching, and healing in order to spread the good news of God's kingdom. The Acts of the Apostles picks up the story from a Lukan perspective to show that the early church did the same thing. The apostles, once emboldened by the Holy Spirit at Pentecost, could not contain their joy at proclaiming the message of Jesus Christ. Major figures, in particular, provide the focus of this urgency, like Peter, Paul, James, Barnabas, and Silas, to name only a few.

Implementing the New Evangelization

The reader might, at this point, be wondering what all this talk about the new evangelization really means in practical terms. Two aspects loom particularly large, it seems to me. One is to ask concretely what is to be expected of Catholics, both individually and collectively, to respond to this urgent call to mission. The second aspect is to pose some realistic questions, primarily revolving around the challenges of the new evangelization. Let's try to address both of these issues briefly here.

When Pope Benedict issued his short *motu proprio* on the Year of Faith in October 2011, it was accompanied by another document to which little attention was drawn. It was a short Note with Pastoral Recommendations for the Year of Faith that came from the Congregation for the Doctrine of the Faith, under the leadership of Cardinal William Levada, who at the time was the prefect of that Congregation. His Note included a series of recommendations on various levels of the church, in particular, the levels of the universal church, episcopal conferences (i.e., conferences of bishops in geographic regions), dioceses, and the local levels (i.e., parishes, communities, and associations). Among the concrete recommendations on the first two levels of the universal church and episcopal conferences, one finds the following:

- participating in the Year of Faith, with pilgrimages, conferences, symposia, study days, and local synods, retreats, days of recollection, and other special events;
- participating in World Youth Day, which is usually held every three years (and most recently took place in July 2013 in Rio de Janeiro, Brazil);

- finding ways to help Catholics deepen their knowledge of the *Catechism of the Catholic Church*, its *Compendium*, and the documents of Vatican Council II;
- encouraging priests to preach on various aspects or themes of evangelization and the transmission of the faith;
- using all possible means of modern communication to get the apostolic message out to the general public, such as radio, television, the internet, Twitter, DVDs, publications of brochures and books, catechetical materials, and the like, and asking Catholic educators, theologians, seminaries, and universities to engage in disseminating information on the new evangelization;
- inviting local bishops (of conferences of bishops) to write pastoral letters on themes related to faith and evangelization;
- encouraging consecrated religious, many of whose communities have been involved in missionary work as well as contemplative prayer, to focus their energies on the new evangelization;
- encouraging outreach in ecumenical and interfaith dialogue, including the model of the "courtyard of the Gentiles" for nonbelievers.

In addition, the document says that for the closing of the Year of Faith, there will be a large celebration with the Holy Father in Rome, affording all members of the church an occasion to profess the faith anew. (Of course, this will now await the decision of Pope Francis.)

Most readers of this book, however, are probably interested more practically in how they might personally participate in the new evangelization on a local level. The aforementioned Note also addresses strategies for parishes and other local communities, including the following:

- improving the quality of one's own relationship with Jesus Christ, through prayer, reflection, and sharing of faith;
- reading the primary documents associated with the Year of Faith and the new evangelization, including the documents of Vatican II and the *Catechism of the Catholic Church* and its *Compendium* (see appendix B);
- increasing participation in the Eucharist and other liturgical celebrations throughout the year, especially the sacrament of reconciliation;

- participating in parish "missions" that go to foreign countries to help with various projects, especially among the poor (such as constructing housing, distributing medicine, teaching catechetics, etc.);
- participating in one or another diocesan or national conference, congress, symposium, or other event that focuses on the new evangelization;
- more willingly sharing one's own experience of faith (i.e., bearing witness) in the context of one's own family, friends, acquaintances, parish, or other group.

As you can see from the above two lists, there is no lack of ideas or opportunities. Most of us, however, have both limited time and resources. So more practically, what can we do?

At the risk of being too limited in my own approach, I would like to propose a few added practical suggestions that should be within the reach of the average parish or parishioner. So I suggest the following considerations:

- Identify just one way in which you might improve your own ability to share your faith with others (lifestyle change? more prayer? attend church? reaching out to the poor, hungry, homeless?).
- Buy a Bible (or study Bible, like the *Little Rock Catholic Study Bible* [published by Liturgical Press] or other edition) and use it; read the Bible five to ten minutes a day, alone or with others; ideally, take a few minutes to share with others your understanding of the text.
- Join or start a Bible study program, perhaps focusing on the gospels or the letters of Paul.
- Subscribe to a journal that encourages *lectio divina* and preparation for the liturgical readings of the week, such as *Give Us This Day* (published by Liturgical Press, http://www.giveusthisday.org/) or *The Word Among Us* (www.wau.org).
- Organize a neighborhood or parish-based potluck dinner/discussion, with the goal of sharing some of your religious faith with others.
- Take the time to read bit by bit a short document like *Porta Fidei* or even a longer document like *Verbum Domini* (these are easily available on the internet through the Vatican website, www.vatican.va).

- Explore responsible Catholic online resources for materials, such as www.usccb.org (the US bishops' website), http://catholic-resources .org (maintained by Jesuit Father Felix Just, SJ), www.americamagazine .org (the weekly national magazine *America*).
- Use this little book for group discussion with some family, friends, or fellow parishioners (it can easily be digested chapter by chapter, allowing for reflection and discussion).
- Ask your local parish to create a few occasions in the year for faith sharing, such as after Sunday Mass or one evening during the week.
- If your local bishop has written a pastoral letter on a given theme for the Year of Faith or for the new evangelization, make that a focus of a group reflection (in the absence of a local pastoral letter, one of the documents referenced in this book would suffice).
- Hold at least one family meal a week, which begins and ends with a prayer, and at which part of the conversation centers around some religious theme.

These lists are obviously intended to be suggestions. Readers can perhaps be even more concrete and creative with their own ideas. Most important, if you value your faith, is that you consider doing something out of the ordinary. We need to stay realistic, of course, and not attempt too much. The new evangelization nonetheless calls each and every one of us to take some personal responsibility for transmitting the faith.

With these more practical suggestions out of the way, we need to turn to some serious challenges that remain for the new evangelization. I suggest that at least five are worthy of some further reflection.

Challenges for the New Evangelization

(1) The first challenge concerns the need for humility. Several synod participants called for a more humble and less triumphant attitude among Catholics when approaching the new evangelization because past efforts at evangelization had sometimes come across in an arrogant fashion, thus paradoxically turning people away from the faith rather than enticing them toward it. This is an ever-present challenge for us Catholics because we are confident indeed that we have the truth. I also think this means asking realistic questions about why so many Christians or Catholics have

become lax in the practice of the faith or abandoned it. Have we at times, whether willingly or by chance, contributed to this reality? Is there more that can be done to limit this "leakage" in the future?

Some Catholics go so far as to suggest that "error has no rights" and that we consequently have no responsibility to engage those whose view of the faith differs from ours or perhaps even from the church's authoritative understanding. But this does not mean we can or should arrogantly impose our faith on others. As Proposition 13 of the synod reminds us, the Gospel of Jesus Christ can never be "imposed" but only "proposed." Our attitude toward the faith can attract people or turn them away. Yes, we must evangelize. Yes, we must be bold in proclaiming the message of salvation in Jesus Christ that we believe in, but we must do it humbly and joyfully. If we do not, we risk repeating errors from the past.

(2) A second challenge is also focused on our own disposition. The real task of evangelization is not merely putting into words our faith but, more importantly, putting it into action. Actually, it is not Paul, perhaps, but the Letter of James that says this best, in a passage cited by Pope Benedict XVI in *Porta Fidei*:

> What good is it, my brothers and sisters, if you say you have faith but do not have works? Can faith save you? If a brother or sister is naked and lacks daily food, and one of you says to them, "Go in peace; keep warm and eat your fill," and yet you do not supply their bodily needs, what is the good of that? So faith by itself, if it has no works, is dead. But someone will say, "You have faith and I have works." Show me your faith apart from your works, and I by my works will show you my faith. (Jas 2:14-18; see *Porta Fidei* 14)

We can speak about our faith all we want, but if our actions do not match our words, we will be empty preachers and the new evangelization will go nowhere. To quote Paul, we would be like noisy gongs or clanging cymbals (1 Cor 13:1).

Francis of Assisi reputedly said, "Preach always. When necessary, use words." That should be a call to the right attitude for the new evangelization. Actions speak far louder than words. That is why all of us members of the church, all of us followers of Jesus, need to be better at implementing more effectively the faith we profess. The biggest weakness in the church is often the failure of its members to live up to the high standards to which we so willingly call others! Essentially, this challenge goes back to what we said earlier. The message of the new evangelization must first be taken to heart by those of us *inside* the faith community, if we want to show those *outside* the value of our faith (see chap. 6 above).

(3) A third challenge of the new evangelization is the need to recall that there is a hierarchy of truths in the Catholic faith. This principle appears at Vatican Council II in relationship to ecumenical outreach to other Christians (*Unitatis Redintegratio* 11). It does not mean that some elements of the faith are optional or less true, but that some are less central than others. Many Catholics mistakenly think every teaching of the church is on the same level. This is not so. For instance, the doctrine of the Trinity or the divinity of Jesus Christ are absolutely essential to the Catholic faith, whereas the validity of appearances of the Virgin Mary are less central. There are also differences in formal teachings. Ecumenical councils are obviously of the highest authority (as well as "dogmatic" constitutions), as are proclaimed dogmas of the faith. But some papal teachings, such as discourses at general audiences or even *motu proprios*, are less essential. The point is that Catholics recognize the need for growth in their faith over time. In fact, the church's own understanding and expression of the faith changes over time, acknowledging the possibility for deepening our understanding of the mysteries that come from God in the faith.

The point of all this is to recall the challenge of remaining flexible in the face of modern challenges to the new evangelization. If we become too narrow in our approach, we may risk offending rather than attracting people.

Let me use an example from Paul. At Corinth, one of the issues he had to address was the issue of meat that had been sacrificed to idols. Remember that Jewish food laws were rather strict and prohibited eating such meat used in pagan ceremonies and then put on the open market. Paul had come to terms with this (and according to Acts, so had Saint Peter; see Acts 10:9-16) in recognizing that certain aspects of the Jewish law (circumcision and the food laws) were not essential with regard to his Gentile converts, though they remained essential for Jews. So it is interesting to see Paul's flexibility at Corinth, where he had to confront the issue of some people giving offense by their eating idol meat. It caused scandal among some in the community, while others saw no problem. Paul's basic principle was rather flexible: "Therefore, if food causes my brother or sister to sin, I will never eat meat again, so that I may not be the cause of them sinning" (1 Cor 8:13, author's translation). Paul's point is clear. There is a greater principle at stake than adhering to or ignoring the food laws. The potential impact of one's behavior also is important.

In other words, especially in the context of the diverse cultures of our age, we need to maintain a certain adaptability in communicating the faith, while never compromising on the essentials.

(4) A fourth challenge is one related to a long tradition of defending the Catholic faith called apologetics. Apologetics is the formal defense and explanation of the faith. It is an ancient tradition, which has seen a rebirth in modern times. Although it is a valid approach to the faith and can contribute greatly to a proper defense of it, we have to be careful with how we use it. It has sometimes been employed as a kind of intellectual "club" to attack or beat down opponents, all in the name of defending the truth. The result has often been to create even further tension or division. Today some take refuge in apologetics as a way to defend every single teaching or practice of the church, especially by using the Scriptures as "proof texts"—passages used literally to prove a point. This approach takes on a very defensive attitude. Moreover, it seems to me that apologetics never convinces those who are irredeemably opposed to the truth, and it is never really needed for those who are already "members of the fold."

One of the strengths of the Second Vatican Council, which set most of the foundations for the new evangelization, was that it did not adopt a strictly apologetic viewpoint. It was neither overly defensive nor offensive. It attempted simply to state the truth of the Catholic faith in a noncontroversial or nonargumentative way. It also avoided words of condemnation of other Christians. Indeed, the council explicitly reached out to other denominations and other faiths, and even to the modern world itself, in order to present the truth of Christ as an invitation. Used properly, apologetics can help explain the basics of the faith, but used as a debate tool with perceived "enemies," it tends to reduce the mysteries of God to purely rational terms. We should, then, be careful when using apologetics in the new evangelization.

(5) A fifth challenge concerns the need for balance in the new evangelization. On the one hand, as Cardinal Wuerl insisted at the end of the synod, the new evangelization is not simply a program. Nor is it just a series of steps or a set of strategies to be implemented. It is about a radical

change of heart on the part of believers, and a new energy directed toward a double outreach, both to those whose faith has become lukewarm or even dead (*ad intra*) and to the world at large (*ad extra*). Ultimately, it is a call to a rediscovery of the faith, which relies on the power of the Holy Spirit and God's own grace to make the message fall on "good ground" where it may grow and flourish. On the other hand, we ourselves must actually engage the new evangelization. Prayer is essential, but so is work. We have to do something. We cannot simply say we will sit back and let God do it. Evangelization takes witnesses. Bearing witness requires faith. Coming to faith means accepting the outstretched hand of God's friendship in Jesus Christ and letting it change our entire worldview.

This is a carefully balanced endeavor, one that recognizes God's initiative *and* our cooperation. Both are needed—grace and human ingenuity. Maintaining the balance is not easy, but I believe it must be done if we are to truly let the new evangelization take hold. It is an act of surrender once more to God's grace at work in our lives and, at the same time, a willingness to engage this divine offer and make it effective.

Paul recognized both aspects in the faith life of his communities. He constantly drew attention to God's grace, the free gift that God had bestowed on humanity through Christ. He also regularly called them to improve their ethical lives, that is, to put their faith in action. Action, of course, also implies love. For, there is no greater proof that our faith is producing good fruit than when it is evident in the love that we show our neighbor (see 1 Cor 13).

Pope Benedict XVI eloquently drew attention to this point in *Porta Fidei* by quoting two passages from Paul (*Porta Fidei* 6 and 7). He cites Paul's notion of "faith working through love" (Gal 5:6) and the passage we saw earlier, *caritas Christi urget nos* ("the love of Christ impels us"; 2 Cor 5:14). In drawing attention to the love needed for the new missionary effort of the new evangelization, the pope wrote,

> Faith grows when it is lived as an experience of love received and when it is communicated as an experience of grace and joy. It makes us fruitful, because it expands our hearts in hope and enables us to bear life-giving witness: indeed, it opens the hearts and minds of those who listen to [and] respond to the Lord's invitation to adhere to his word and become his disciples. (*Porta Fidei* 7)

The new evangelization cannot succeed if the mission is not embraced with love. But with love, it will not fail. Moreover, if faith is proclaimed with love, it also leads to hope, the third virtue in the great triad of virtues proclaimed by Paul in the Christian tradition (1 Cor 13:13). People who are filled with hope, even in spite of very difficult circumstances surrounding them, are never deluded by the apparent failure of their efforts. Evangelization can never be reduced to success in numbers or the awesome effect of big, expansive programs that wow people with attractive displays (see IL 74). Hope is based upon the quiet, interior disposition that says, "God is in charge."

These five are not the only challenges for the new evangelization, but they seem to me to be rather urgent ones. They can serve as warnings that we should approach the task of the new evangelization with care. We will need open, humble, joyful, loving hearts to put this bold vision into action. We must also always remain vigilant to avoid the pitfalls that can become true stumbling blocks in evangelization efforts.

A Parting Look at Paul the Evangelizer

To conclude this chapter, I want to revisit Paul once more. One of my senior confreres, a well-known and prolific French theologian by the name of René Coste, recently wrote a book on friendship with Jesus in which he calls Paul "the one passionately attached to Christ." His reflections are so on the mark that I feel compelled here to cite his summary of Paul's passionate ministry of evangelization:

> It suffices to note how dedicated [Paul] was to proclaiming the Gospel, sparing no energy, confronting a series of grave trials, of which he left us a list in the Second Letter to the Corinthians (cf. 11:21-28). Moreover, it is he who writes: "I do it all for the sake of the Gospel" (1 Cor 9:23), exercising with unreserved generosity what he called "anxiety for the Churches" (2 Cor 11:28). We see a commitment that can only be explained by a soul truly fascinated by the light of the Gospel, in love with Christ, a soul sustained by profound conviction; it is necessary to bring Christ's light to the world, to proclaim the Gospel to all of us. This seems to me to be what remains for us, . . . to see his passion for the Gospel and thereby grasp the greatness, the beauty, indeed the deep need of

the Gospel for all of us. Let us pray the Lord who caused St Paul to see his light, who made him hear his word and profoundly moved his heart, that we may also see his light, so that our hearts too may be moved by his Word and thus that we too may give the light of the Gospel and the truth of Christ to today's world which thirsts for it. (René Coste, *L'amitié avec Jésus* [Paris: Cerf, 2012], 306; author's translation)

To my mind, this expresses well the "spirit" of the new evangelization and why Paul is such a good model for it.

Review and Reflection Questions

1. In New Testament times, why was evangelization considered an urgent matter? Do you think the urgency for this mission still exists today?

2. How would you describe the relationship between faith and love? How does hope enter this relationship? Why are these three virtues given preeminence in the New Testament?

3. Realistically, can you identify one or two personal strategies for yourself, your family, or your friends that would make the task of the new evangelization appealing and possible?

4. Why do you think some Christians, even Catholics, abandon their faith or become lax in living it out? What can be done to help keep people faithful in practicing the Christian faith?

Conclusion

We have come to the end of our exploration of the new evangelization in light of Paul's letters. It is an appropriate point to review briefly what we have tried to accomplish.

After an introduction and explanation of how synods function, I suggested that there are at least the following six primary characteristics of the new evangelization:

- personalistic and Christocentric;
- seeks a rediscovery of the church's missionary spirit;
- both outwardly oriented to the world and inwardly to believers;
- targeted to individuals and whole cultures;
- not merely for professional missionaries but all the baptized;
- envisions an entire process of Christianization.

I then suggested that we could find good support in the letters of Saint Paul for all of these characteristics. I went on to add several more features found in the letters that are pertinent to the new evangelization. I treated them in various sections of the book:

- the urgency of the mission of evangelization;
- individual and communal dimensions of the faith;
- the call for ongoing conversion;
- multiple means to sustain the new evangelization, especially prayer, the Sacred Scriptures, the sacraments, a commitment to justice and peace, and ethics;
- the primacy of love over all other virtues.

Along the way, I also pointed out some cautions with regard to the new evangelization and drew attention to some realistic concerns.

These are hardly the only ways to describe the new evangelization; nor do they present an overview of Paul's own thought. Rather, they are intended to be a kind of schema, an overarching way of conceiving the new evangelization that is rooted in Sacred Scripture, especially the figure of Paul, and that also engages contemporary challenges.

Paul would hardly be the only good model for the new evangelization, even if the characteristics we have addressed are at home in his worldview. Other models have been proposed, such as Saint Augustine, or Saint Stephen, or Saints Cyril and Methodius. For that matter, almost all the martyrs could be proposed as models because they paid the highest price of all for evangelization, giving their own lives for the sake of the faith. This is all the more pertinent when recalling that the Greek root of the word martyr means to "bear witness." It is the primary New Testament word for transmitting the faith by deed, and not merely by word.

Jesus himself, of course, is the first evangelizer, the model of models (IL 21–24). The gospels show him ceaselessly going forth to proclaim the good news of God's kingdom. Most of us, however, would be a bit reluctant to propose that we are immediately worthy of following his example so perfectly. What I like about Paul as a model for the new evangelization is that he is one of the real, concrete "characters" from Scripture. His humanity, like our own, stands out. He came with many gifts, but he also had his faults, as do all the saints. Life was not always easy for him or for his communities. Yet given Paul's powerful legacy as apostle and evangelizer, I think we can do well to take him and his message to heart when trying to implement the new evangelization, for ourselves, our parishes, our dioceses, and our church.

No one can predict exactly what Pope Francis will do with this vision of the new evangelization, although his past ministry as a bishop has demonstrated his strong interest in the topic and his affirmation of the teachings from Aparecida. What is clear is that the Year of Faith, in conjunction with the 2012 synod, was only a beginning point. The new evangelization is a long-term enterprise that could engage the church for many years to come. If it is not to fizzle out, we will all be called to work diligently at implementing what may seem like a rather exalted vision. Like Paul, if we recall that God's grace is pulling us forward, and that our cooperation with this grace is urgently needed, I remain hopeful that we can make the new evangelization an effective tool in spreading the Gospel of Jesus Christ in the twenty-first century.

Mary, Star of the New Evangelization

I want to conclude with another model, which is found in the synod's documents, and suggest, perhaps a bit creatively, there may be a slight connection to Paul. Primary among the proposed models for the new evangelization is Mary, the mother of Jesus and mother of the church. As has become very frequent in official church teachings, several documents on the new evangelization invoke the image of the Virgin Mary, mother of Jesus, as a guiding light for this process. On this score, Saint Paul may seem a bit lacking. Paul never mentions Mary by name in his letters. His only mention of the mother of Jesus is a passing remark in the letter to the Galatians, where he recalls that Jesus was "born of a woman" (Gal 4:4). This phrase is used in the context of underlining the humanity of Jesus, his full participation in human existence by being born into this world through a woman, as all human beings are.

This may be a minimal recognition by the Apostle, but we must remember Marian piety, as we now understand it in the church, evolved only gradually over the centuries. Paul's brief acknowledgment of her role in Jesus' existence is sufficient to show his acceptance of her role. Had Paul been familiar with Luke's gospel, for instance, which came much later, I think Paul would have been quite happy to acknowledge Mary as a good model for discipleship. She both heard and accomplished God's Word in her life (Luke 1:38, 46, 49). Moreover, Paul's letters clearly show Paul's ability to work with many women in ministry and to recognize their contribution to the proclamation of the Gospel.

Be that as it may, both the Final Message of the synod and the final proposition present Mary as a model for the new evangelization (Final Message 14 and Prop. 58). She is the "star of the new evangelization" whose light brightens the desert of our modern existence. She is a model missionary who bore the Word made flesh into the world and who gave witness to his greatness by her own humility. To entrust the new evangelization to her guidance and protection is simply to entrust ourselves once more to a gentle, loving, and humble mother who wants only the best for her children. In fact, Paul intriguingly compared himself to a loving mother with regard to his own communities (1 Thess 2:7; Gal 4:19), so perhaps intuitively he was simply mirroring what later generations would acknowledge more explicitly in Mary's supporting role in the history of salvation.

So as we conclude this exercise in bringing Paul and the new evangelization together, I too invoke the guidance of Mary, who in her own humble way has shown us the path to respond to this new call to become missionary disciples in our own day. May her star shine brightly on the church's enterprise, and may all that we do as new evangelizers help lead others to her Son, by the power of the Holy Spirit, and to the glory of the Father! That is, I believe, what both she and Paul the Apostle would want.

Prayer for the New Evangelization

Several special prayers have been composed for the new evangelization. I offer here one proposed by the United States Conference of Catholic Bishops.

> *"'Everyone who calls on the name of the Lord will be saved.' But how can they call on him in whom they have not believed? And how can they believe in him of whom they have not heard? And how can they hear without someone to preach? And how can people preach unless they are sent?" —Romans 10:13-15 (NAB)*

Heavenly Father,

Pour forth your Holy Spirit to inspire me with these words from Holy Scripture.

Stir in my soul the desire to renew my faith and deepen my relationship with your Son, our Lord Jesus Christ so that I might truly believe in and live the Good News.

Open my heart to hear the Gospel and grant me the confidence to proclaim the Good News to others.

Pour out your Spirit, so that I might be strengthened to go forth and witness to the Gospel in my everyday life through my words and actions.

In moments of hesitation, remind me:

If not me, then who will proclaim the Gospel?

If not now, then when will the Gospel be proclaimed?

If not the truth of the Gospel, then what shall I proclaim?

God, our Father, I pray that through the Holy Spirit I might hear the call of the New Evangelization to deepen my faith, grow in confidence to proclaim the Gospel and boldly witness to the saving grace of your Son, Jesus Christ, who lives and reigns with you, in the unity of the Holy Spirit, one God, for ever and ever.

Amen.

Glossary

ad extra: Latin for "outwardly," designating the church's traditional missionary stance, outwardly directing the message to those who have yet to hear the Gospel of Jesus Christ

ad gentes: Latin for "to the world" or "to the peoples"; a shortened form of the expression *missio ad gentes* used to designate the church's mission to proclaim the good news of Jesus Christ to the world at large, especially nonbelievers; also serves as the title of Vatican II's Decree on the Church's Missionary Activity (*Ad Gentes Divinitus*; Dec. 7, 1965)

ad intra: Latin for "inwardly," designating the evangelical task of proclaiming the Gospel message to those already in the church

aggiornamento: Italian for "bringing up to date" or "renewal"; used by Pope John XXIII to explain the main purpose of convoking an ecumenical council in order to make the truths of the faith more comprehensible in a modern context

apologetics: From Greek *apologia* (justification, defense), the art of explaining and defending the faith by use of human reasoning and careful exposition of the Bible and church teachings; this was a characteristic of earlier periods of church history, especially the Patristic era and the Middle Ages

apostolic exhortation: A document written and promulgated by a pope on a specific topic; recent popes have regularly produced these after a synod (postsynodal) as a formal teaching resulting from the synod of bishops; *Verbum Domini* (2010) was a postsynodal apostolic exhortation of Pope Benedict XVI that came from the 2008 synod on the Word of God

Apostolic See (also Holy See): Proper name for the Diocese of Rome, governed by the pope, now representing the authority of the pope to govern the church as the successor of the apostle Peter

areopaghi: The plural form of Areopagus, a name for a hill in ancient Athens (the Hill of Ares) or the governing council of Athens, which used to meet on the hill; Paul once preached at the Areopagus (Acts 16:22-34); the expression now serves as an image for Christians boldly encountering nonbelievers on their own turf and engaging them in dialogue

catechism, catechesis, catechize, catechetics: From Greek *katechizein* (to teach by mouth); a concise summary or compendium of official church teaching, often in question-answer format; the act of teaching the basic truths of a religion; the content of such teaching

Christocentric: Literally, Christ-centered; making Jesus Christ and his significance the primary focus of one's teaching

consistory: A special meeting of cardinals, who function like an inner "senate" for the pope, called irregularly by the pope, usually to create new cardinals or to consult with the cardinals on various urgent matters in the church

courtyard of the Gentiles: A special area of the Jewish temple in Jerusalem where non-Jews were allowed to congregate; it now serves as a metaphor or biblical image for formal encounters or dialogues between believers and nonbelievers

Curia: From Latin, originally meaning a subdivision of a tribe, it is the name given to the group of Roman congregations (offices or dicasteries) of the Holy See (Vatican) that help the pope govern the Catholic Church

dicastery (pl. dicasteries): From Greek *dikastērion* (court of law); technical word for a department of the Holy See, such as the various congregations, pontifical councils, tribunals, or other bodies of the Vatican's administrative structure

didache, didactic: From Greek *didachē* (teaching); can represent (a) the act of teaching or (b) the content of teaching; used in the New Testament of formal teaching(s) and distinguished from preaching

ecclesiology, ecclesiological: From Greek *ekklēsia* and *logos*, meaning the study of the church

ecumenical: From Greek *oikoumenē* (inhabited world), referring to (a) worldwide gatherings of authorities such as a council or (b) interdenominational meetings or relations

encyclical: An authoritative letter issued by the pope on a given theme; this practice became more frequent among popes of the nineteenth and twentieth centuries

evangelization: From Greek *euaggelizai, euaggelion* (to announce good news); used of the church's apostolic mission to proclaim the faith worldwide

Holy See: See *Apostolic See*

incarnation, incarnate, incarnational(ly): From Latin *in* and *caro* (flesh), literally "enfleshment"; the dogma of the eternal Word (Christ) becoming human or taking on human flesh (see John 1:14)

Instrumentum Laboris: Latin, "working document"; the document prepared for a synod of bishops by the Pontifical Council for Synods of Bishops, usually after wide consultation with bishops and experts from around the world

kerygma: From Greek *kēryssein* (to announce, proclaim, preach, make known); can represent (a) the act of proclaiming the good news of the Gospel or (b) the content of this proclamation; distinguished from formal teaching (didache)

lectio divina: Latin for "holy or prayerful reading"; ancient practice of slow, prayerful meditation on Sacred Scripture; in the monastic practice this developed especially into the four main steps, *lectio* (reading), *oratio* (oral prayer), *meditatio* (meditation), and *contemplatio* (contemplation), a progressive set of stages to deepen one's understanding of the biblical message

Lineamenta: "Main lines or characteristics," from Latin, *lineare* (to draw a line); a draft document in preparation for a synod of bishops; it is widely circulated in advance to solicit responses and recommendations to help identify major themes or main topics for a synod of bishops

magisterium, magisterial: From Latin *magister* (teacher); the official, living teaching authority of the church

missio ad gentes: See *ad gentes*; the church's mission of proclaiming the Gospel of Jesus Christ to the whole world, based upon Christ's commission to the apostles (Matt 28:18-20)

motu proprio: Latin, "on his own authority"; used for papal teachings that are of lesser authority than encyclicals but nonetheless authoritatively address certain issues or call for certain actions and are issued by the pope's own authority

propositions: From Latin *propositiones*; formal decisions/recommendations of a synod sent to the pope for his consideration in preparing a final document to express the outcome of a synod

Relatio ante disceptationem: Latin, "report before the discussion"; presentation given at the beginning of a synod by the relator general in order to give direction to the work of the synod and help set its agenda

Relatio post disceptationem: Latin, "report after the discussion"; the discourse given by the relator general at the end of a synod to pull together the principal ideas of the synod to focus drawing up the propositions

relator general: The bishop or cardinal appointed by the pope to oversee the opening and closing of a synod of bishops; Cardinal Donald Wuerl, archbishop of Washington, served in this capacity at the 2012 synod on the new evangelization for the transmission of the Christian faith

Septuagint: From Greek, meaning "seventy," and often abbreviated with the Roman numeral LXX; this is the Greek translation of the Hebrew Bible, which tradition says was accomplished by seventy scholars working independently to adapt the Hebrew text for Jews living in the Diaspora who were in danger of losing command of their native languages of Hebrew and Aramaic; this edition of the Old Testament became the basis for the Catholic canon of the Old Testament

synod (of bishops): Established by Pope Paul VI near the end of Vatican II as a consultative body for the pope, this assembly of bishop-delegates from around the world meets periodically in ordinary or extraordinary sessions to study given topics of current importance in the church; synods often produce a postsynodal document on the theme studied

theology, theological: From Greek *theos* and *logos*, meaning the study of God; can refer narrowly to (a) the specific view or analysis of God in biblical or church documents or, more broadly, to (b) a religious outlook

Vulgate: From Latin for "common," this was the Latin translation of the Bible from the original languages of Hebrew and Greek, initiated by Saint Jerome (ca. 340–ca. 420), who revised older Latin editions of the gospels to make the Bible more accessible to the Latin-speaking people of his day

Appendix A

Synods of Bishops in the Catholic Church since Vatican II

Year	Number	Type	Theme	Final Document
1967	I	Ordinary General	Preserving and strengthening the Catholic faith in the wake of Vatican II	None published
1969		Extraordinary General	Cooperation between the Holy See and episcopal conferences	None published
1971	II	Ordinary General	The ministerial priesthood and social justice	Justice in the World (1971); The Ministerial Priesthood (1971)
1974	III	Ordinary General	Evangelization in the modern world in the wake of Vatican II	*Evangelii Nuntiandi* (1975), postsynodal apostolic exhortation of Pope Paul VI
1977	IV	Ordinary General	Catechesis	*Catechesi Tradendae* (1979), postsynodal apostolic exhortation of Pope John Paul II
1980		Special	The Netherlands	Conclusion (1980)
1980	V	Ordinary General	The Christian family	*Familiaris Consortio* (1981), postsynodal apostolic exhortation of Pope John Paul II

Year	Number	Type	Theme	Final Document
1983	VI	Ordinary General	Penance and reconciliation	*Reconciliatio et Paenitentia* (1984), postsynodal apostolic exhortation of Pope John Paul II
1985		Extraordinary General	20th anniversary of Vatican Council II and how to interpret it	Final Report (1985)
1987	VII	Ordinary General	The role of the lay faithful in the church and the world	*Christifidelis Laici* (1988), postsynodal apostolic exhortation of Pope John Paul II
1990	VIII	Ordinary General	Priestly formation	*Pastores Dabo Vobis* (1992), postsynodal apostolic exhortation of Pope John Paul II
1991		Special	Europe (I)	None
1994		Special	Africa (I)	*Ecclesia in Africa* (1995)
1994	IX	Ordinary General	Consecrated life	*Vita Consecrata* (1996), postsynodal apostolic exhortation of Pope John Paul II
1995		Special	Lebanon	*Ecclesia in Lebanon* (1997), postsynodal apostolic exhortation of Pope John Paul II
1997		Special	America	*Ecclesia in America* (1999), postsynodal apostolic exhortation of Pope John Paul II
1998		Special	Asia	*Ecclesia in Asia* (1999), postsynodal apostolic exhortation of Pope John Paul II
1998		Special	Oceania	*Ecclesia in Oceania* (2001), postsynodal apostolic exhortation of Pope John Paul II

Year	Number	Type	Theme	Final Document
1999		Special	Europe (II)	*Ecclesia in Europa* (2003), postsynodal apostolic exhortation of Pope John Paul II
2001	X	Ordinary General	Role of bishops in the church	*Pastores Gregis* (2003), postsynodal apostolic exhortation of Pope John Paul II
2005	XI	Ordinary General	The Eucharist	*Sacramentum Caritatis* (2007), postsynodal apostolic exhortation of Pope Benedict XVI
2008	XII	Ordinary General	The Word of God	*Verbum Domini* (2010), postsynodal apostolic exhortation of Pope Benedict XVI
2009		Special	Africa (II)	*Africae Munus* (2011), postsynodal apostolic exhortation of Pope Benedict XVI
2010		Special	The Middle East	*Ecclesia in Medio Oriente* (2012), postsynodal apostolic exhortation of Pope Benedict XVI
2012	XIII	Ordinary General	New evangelization for the transmission of the Christian faith	*Lumen Fidei*, encyclical letter of Pope Francis, July 5, 2013; a postsynodal apostolic exhortation on the new evangelization will also likely be forthcoming

Pope Paul VI established the Synod of Bishops with his *motu proprio, Apostolica Sollicitudo,* published in 1965, only months before the end of the Second Vatican Council. He defined the purpose of the synod as follows:

> It is an ecclesiastic institution, which, on interrogating the signs of the times and as well as trying to provide a deeper interpretation of divine designs and the constitution of the Catholic Church, we set up after Vatican Council II in order to foster the unity and cooperation of bishops around the world with the Holy See. It does this by means of a common study concerning the conditions of the church and a joint solution on matters concerning her mission. It is neither a council nor a parliament but a special type of synod. (Sunday *Angelus* of September 22, 1974)

The Code of Canon Law defines the Synod of Bishops with these words:

> The synod of bishops is that group of bishops who have been chosen from different regions of the world and who meet at stated times to foster a closer unity between the Roman Pontiff and the bishops, to assist the Roman Pontiff with their counsel in safeguarding and increasing faith and morals and in preserving and strengthening ecclesiastical discipline, and to consider questions concerning the Church's activity in the world. (*Code of Canon Law: Latin-English Edition* [Washington, DC: Canon Law Society of America, 1983], c. 342)

Thus, the synod is a consultative body of representative bishops to help the pope in the governance of the church. Both Pope John Paul II and Pope Benedict XVI subsequently refined the design and functioning of the synod through legislation of their own.

Since its foundation, there have been twenty-five synods, to date. They are classed in three categories. The most basic type is called an "ordinary general" synod, held on a regular basis (originally intended to be every two years, then revised to every three or four years) to address current issues in the church.

The second type is the "extraordinary general" synod, which is called by the pope only to address particular or urgent themes. The synod of 1985, for instance, was convened to celebrate the twentieth anniversary of the Second Vatican Council. Its concluding document lays out several important criteria for interpreting the nature of that council.

The third type of synod is labeled a "special" assembly. These are convened to address the unique concerns of specific geographic regions in the church. Pope John Paul II held a number of these in preparation for the third Christian millennium. So far, there have been thirteen ordinary general synods, ten special synods, and only two extraordinary general synods. There was also an extraordinary synod of bishops for Ukrainian Catholic bishops (1980), but this falls outside our consideration.

Although a few synods have issued their own final documents (notably 1971), John Paul II uniformly began issuing concluding documents at some point after the synods ended, using information from the synods but publishing the final teaching in his own name. Benedict XVI continued this practice, but a future pope could decide otherwise. Some theological experts point out that despite the ancient custom of synods in the church, the modern practice has been turned into another vehicle for papal teaching rather than a true teaching organ on its own on behalf of the college of bishops. This is seen in the current practice of submitting propositions to the Holy Father at a synod's conclusion, so that he may use them in formulating a final message.

There is a separate office in the Roman Curia called the Synod of Bishops, which oversees the ongoing work of the synod under the supervision of a general secretary and staff. One can find many of the documents in the chart, as well as other preparatory documents and related materials, on the Vatican website (http://www.vatican.va/roman_curia /synod/index.htm).

Appendix B
Major Church Resource Documents for the New Evangelization

This chart only includes the most important magisterial documents that have directly influenced the project of the new evangelization from the universal level of the church. They are listed here in *reverse chronological order*, beginning with the most recent documents, and then extending backwards to other influential church teachings in recent decades. Other documents issued in conjunction with the great jubilee of the third Christian millennium have not been included. Nor have I included documents from local episcopal conferences or churches, some of which are well done. See, for example, the US bishops' statement Called to Be Disciples: The New Evangelization (Washington, DC: USCCB, 2012), which was produced by the Bishops' Committee on Evangelization and Catechesis.

Document Title	Type	Outline	Significance	Date
Final propositions	List of the final propositions adopted at the synod and sent to Pope Benedict XVI for his use in preparing a final message (which will perhaps be an apostolic exhortation by Pope Francis)	Introduction I. Nature of the New Evangelization II. Context of the Church's Ministry Today III. Pastoral Responses to the Circumstances of Our Day IV. Agents/Participants of the New Evangelization Conclusion	These propositions normally provide the main input to the pope to write a final instruction, usually an apostolic exhortation, on the synod's theme	October 2012
Instrumentum Laboris	Working document for the synod on the new evangelization	Preface Introduction I. Jesus Christ, the Good News of God to Humanity II. Time for a New Evangelization III. Transmitting the Faith IV. Revivifying Pastoral Activity Conclusion	As the working document of the synod, it provided most of the main themes and directions for the discussions	June 2012

Document Title	Type	Outline	Significance	Date
Motu proprio Porta Fidei	*Motu proprio* of Pope Benedict XVI inaugurating the Year of Faith; was issued with a "Note" from the Congregation for the Doctrine of the Faith on pastoral recommendations	A summons to authentic renewal and conversion in the church	A short (fifteen paragraphs) papal proclamation of the Year of Faith that gave both its rationale and basic orientation; the accompanying "Note" gave many specific pastoral recommendations for the universal, regional (episcopal conferences), diocesan, and local levels	October 2011
Lineamenta	Preparatory document for the synod on the new evangelization	Preface Introduction I. Time for a New Evangelization II. Proclaiming the Gospel of Jesus Christ III. Initiation into the Christian Experience Conclusion	The first document for the synod, it provided a general orientation for gathering more precise and detailed information from the world's bishops in order to formulate a working document for the synod; included dozens of questions for reflection	February 2011
Verbum Domini	Apostolic exhortation of Benedict XVI following the synod on the Word, 2008	Introduction I: *Verbum Dei* (The Word of God) II: *Verbum in Ecclesia* (The Word in the Church) III: *Verbum Mundo* (The Word in the World)	The most important papal statement on Scripture since Vatican Council II, it came from a synod of bishops on the theme of the Word of God	Sept. 30, 2010

Aparecida document	Final document from the fifth assembly of the bishops of Latin America and the Caribbean, May 13–31, 2007, in Aparecida, Brazil	Introduction I: The Life of Our People Today II: The Life of Jesus Christ in Missionary Disciples III: The Life of Jesus Christ for Our Peoples Conclusion	A very lengthy final teaching from the fifth general assembly of Latin American bishops, which was also attended by Pope Benedict XVI; it provides a master plan for the new evangelization in Latin and South America (a "continental mission"); a strong call for everyone at all levels in the church to become "missionary disciples"	June 29, 2008
Doctrinal Note on Some Aspects of Evangelization	An instruction from the Congregation for the Doctrine of the Faith, with the approval of Pope Benedict XVI	I. Introduction II. Some Anthropological Implications III. Some Ecclesiological Implications IV. Some Ecumenical Implications V. Conclusion	Although issued by a Congregation rather than the pope himself, this technical doctrinal note was intended to explain the Catholic Church's approach to evangelization in light of delicate questions relating to ecumenical dialogues	Dec. 3, 2007
Novo Millennio Ineunte	Apostolic letter of Pope John Paul II at the close of the celebrations for the new millennium	Introduction I. Meeting Christ: The Legacy of the Great Jubilee II. A Face to Contemplate III. Starting Afresh from Christ IV. Witnesses to Love Conclusion: *Duc in Altum* (Go out into the deep!)	A retrospective on the great jubilee year 2000 and how it opened up fresh avenues for the church's mission to proclaim the Gospel message of Christ with renewed vigor	Jan. 6, 2001

Document Title	Type	Outline	Significance	Date
Tertio Millennio Adveniente	Apostolic letter of Pope John Paul II to prepare for the third Christian millennium	Introduction I. "Jesus Christ is the Same Yester- day and Today" (Heb 13:8) II. The Jubilee of the Year 2000 III. Preparation for the Great Jubilee IV. Immediate Preparation V. "Jesus Christ is the Same . . . For- ever" (Heb 13:8)	Proclaimed a three-year preparatory program around the theme of the Trinity to call the church to repen- tance and to urge conversion; Year One on Jesus Christ (1997); Year Two on the Holy Spirit (1998); and Year Three on God the Father (1999)	Nov. 14, 1994
Catechism of the Catholic Church	Compendium of Catholic teach- ing promulgated by Pope John Paul II in the apostolic constitu- tion *Fidei Depositum* (August 15, 1997)	Prologue I: Profession of Faith II: Celebration of the Christian Mystery III: Life in Christ IV: Christian Prayer	The authoritative compendium of Catholic teaching; assembled at the request of Pope John Paul II; the size of the catechism made its use by the average Catholic cumbersome, so other shorter compilations were published to make the document more user-friendly, especially the *Compendium of the Catechism of the Catholic Church* (2005) and *YOUCAT, Youth Catechism of the Catholic Church* (2011) published for World Youth Day	1992; 2nd ed. 1997

Redemptoris Missio	Encyclical letter of Pope John Paul II	Introduction I. Jesus Christ, the Only Savior II. The Kingdom of God III. The Holy Spirit, the Principal Agent of Mission IV. The Vast Horizons of the *Missio ad Gentes* V. The Paths of the Mission VI. Leaders and Workers in the Missionary Apostolate VII. Cooperation in Missionary Activity VIII. Missionary Spirituality	Lengthy and detailed instruction on the urgency of the church's missionary outreach to the world; it provides the basic inspiration for the "new evangelization" as envisioned by Pope John Paul II	Dec. 7, 1990

Document Title	Type	Outline	Significance	Date
Christifi-delis Laici	Apostolic exhortation of Pope John Paul II following the 1987 synod of bishops on the laity	Introduction I: I am the Vine, You Are the Branches: The Dignity of the Lay Faithful in the Church as Mystery II: All Branches of a Single Vine: The Participation of the Lay Faithful in the Life of the Church as Communion III: I Have Appointed You to Go Forth and Bear Fruit: The Coresponsibility of the Lay Faithful in the Church as Mission IV: Laborers in the Lord's Vineyard: Good Stewards of God's Varied Grace V: That You Bear Much Fruit: The Formation of the Lay Faithful in the Lay State	Part of a series on the various roles of members of the church, this lengthy document focuses on the lay faithful, who were also highlighted in Vatican II; the teaching can be seen in connection with *Vita Consecrata* (1996) on religious life, and *Pastores Dabo Vobis* (1992) on the formation of priests	Dec. 30, 1988

Catechesi Tradendae	Apostolic exhortation of Pope John Paul II following the 1977 synod of bishops on catechesis	Introduction I. We Have But One Teacher, Jesus Christ II. An Experience as Old as the Church III. Catechesis in the Church's Pastoral and Missionary Activity IV. The Whole of the Good News Drawn from its Source V. Everybody Needs to be Catechized VI. Some Ways and Means of Catechesis VII. How To Impart Catechesis VIII. The Joy of Faith in a Troubled World IX. The Task Concerns Us All Conclusion	This extensive teaching touches many aspects of the new evangelization and draws attention to the need for good catechesis of all the faithful; it builds upon the personal encounter with Christ and proceeds to the systematic presentation of the Christian faith	Oct. 16, 1979
Evangelii Nuntiandi	Apostolic exhortation of Pope Paul VI following the 1974 synod of bishops on evangelization	Addressed to the bishops, clergy, and laity around the world, this exhortation calls Catholics to renewed efforts at evangelization	This papal document of 79 paragraphs gave impetus to renewed efforts to evangelize for the faith in modern times; it provides much of the inspiration behind John Paul II's vision of the "new evangelization," which has nevertheless evolved in other directions as well	Dec. 8, 1975

Document Title	Type	Outline	Significance	Date
Ad Gentes Divinitus	Vatican Council II's Decree on the Church's Missionary Activity	Introduction I. Doctrinal Principles II. Missionary Work III. Particular Churches IV. Missionaries V. The Organization of Missionary Activity VI. Cooperation	As an authoritative teaching from an ecumenical council, this decree explains the urgency and many aspects of the church's efforts to take the Gospel message of Jesus Christ to the ends of the earth	Dec. 7, 1965
Dei Verbum	Vatican Council II's Dogmatic Constitution on Divine Revelation	Prologue I. Divine Revelation Itself II. The Transmission of Divine Revelation III. Sacred Scripture: Its Divine Inspiration and Its Interpretation IV. The Old Testament V. The New Testament VI. Sacred Scripture in the Life of the Church	As a dogmatic constitution of an ecumenical council, it constitutes the highest authoritative statement on Scripture and divine revelation; although it does not concern evangelization directly, it set the stage for a Catholic understanding of Scripture and provides the rationale for using Scripture in the church's mission, something underscored by *Verbum Domini*	Nov. 18, 1965

Appendix C
Final Message of the Synod on the New Evangelization

October 26, 2012

This twelve-page document was issued near the end of the synod and was intended to be a message of hope and optimism to the entire church. The text was published in various languages and was explained in a press conference presided over by several bishops from the synod, two of whom were to become cardinals on November 24, 2012 (John Olorunfemi Onaiyekan, archbishop of Abuja [Nigeria], and Luis Antonio G. Tagle, archbishop of Manila [Philippines]). Their nomination to become cardinals came just at the conclusion of the synod. Pope Benedict XVI made the surprise announcement of a special consistory to create only six new cardinals, in part, to emphasize the universality of the church. (Only one hailed from North America; the five others were from Asia, Africa, South America, the Middle East, and India.) Later events would show that he was likely also interested in bolstering the number of electors in the College of Cardinals in preparation for his resignation from the papacy at the end of February 2013.

Summary Chart of the Final Message

Par.	Title	Content
1	Like the Samaritan woman at the well	The biblical image of the woman at the well (John 4:5-42) as a symbol of humanity's thirst for the Lord
2	A new evangelization	Uses Paul's exclamation in 1 Corinthians 9:16 for the urgency of the new evangelization
3	The personal encounter with Jesus Christ in the church	A call to a personal encounter with the risen Lord Jesus
4	The occasions of encountering Jesus and listening to the Scriptures	The important role of Scripture in promoting this religious encounter
5	Evangelizing ourselves and opening ourselves to conversion	Emphasizes the "inward" direction of evangelization; all need to be evangelized
6	Seizing new opportunities for evangelization in the world today	A call to confront the new realities of the modern world with the truth of the Gospel message
7	Evangelization, the family, and consecrated life	Underlines the essential role of families and religious women and men in sustaining the faith
8	The ecclesial community and the many agents of evangelization	A universal call of *all* the members of the church to participate in evangelization
9	That the youth may encounter Christ	The unique role the young can play in the faith; they profoundly seek the truth and have high aspirations
10	The Gospel in dialogue with human culture and experience with religions	Promotes the dialogue between faith and reason and the diverse cultural contexts of modern life
11	Remembering the Second Vatican Council and referring to the *Catechism of the Catholic Church* in the Year of Faith	Recalls the anniversaries of Vatican II (50 years ago, 1962–65) and the *Catechism* (20 years ago, 1992)

Par.	Title	Content
12	Contemplating the mystery and being at the side of the poor	Highlights the church's ongoing mission of solidarity with the poor
13	To the churches in the various regions of the world	Affirms the various parts of the church, especially the Catholic Oriental Churches and the unique contexts of each diverse region of the world
14	The star of Mary illumines the desert	Calls upon Mary as a shining star who can lead the way through the "desert" to support the new evangelization

Appendix D

Propositions from the Synod on the New Evangelization

Propo-sition	Topic	Main point(s)
1	Documents Submitted to the Pope	Lists the documents presented to the Holy Father, including the *Lineamenta*, *Instrumentum Laboris*, the relator's presentations at the beginning and close of the synod, the Final Message to the People of God, all the presentations and small group reports; asks the Holy Father to consider publishing a document on the theme of the synod
2	Expression of Gratitude	The thanks of the synod participants for prior teachings of popes, including Pope Benedict XVI, that touch on the theme of evangelization
3	Oriental Catholic Churches	Expresses the gratitude of the Eastern Rite Catholic churches for their participation and for their own heritage and urges better knowledge and respect for these rites
4	The Holy Trinity: Source of the New Evangelization	Acknowledging "the primacy of God's grace," this proposition underlines how the church continues the mission of God's own outreach to humanity as a union of Father, Son, and Spirit
5	New Evangelization and Inculturation	Calls for recognition of the importance of culture in making the faith comprehensible; the faith must be inculturated

Propo-sition	Topic	Main point(s)
6	Proclamation of the Gospel	Emphasizes the Gospel message of universal salvation
7	New Evangelization as Permanent Missionary Dimension of the Church	Reaffirms evangelization as (1) *ad gentes* (i.e., to those not yet converted to Christ); (2) a means to promote growth in faith; and (3) directed to those who already have received the faith but have grown distant from it
8	Witnessing in a Secularized World	Notes the necessity of recognizing the secular world and its influence and the need to proclaim the Gospel message in this context
9	The New Evangelization and Initial Proclamation	Suggests drawing up guidelines or pastoral plan for initial proclamation (Greek, *kerygma*), including church teaching on Scripture and tradition, teachings and quotations from missionaries and martyrs, and qualities and guidelines for contemporary evangelizers
10	Right to Proclaim and to Hear the Gospel	Defends the inalienable human right of people both to announce and receive the Gospel message (see esp. Matt 28:19)
11	New Evangelization and *Lectio Divina*	The only proposition singularly dedicated to Scripture, it suggests the importance of both study and prayerful reading of Scripture; also recommends that "Scripture should permeate homilies"
12	Documents of Vatican II	Reiterates Pope Benedict XVI's call for rereading the documents of Vatican II from the hermeneutical principle of "continuity"
13	Challenges of Our Time	Acknowledges contemporary difficulties in the context of globalization and secularism that make evangelizing precarious, yet the Gospel cannot be "imposed" but only "proposed"
14	New Evangelization and Reconciliation	In the context of world divisions and conflicts, underlines the necessity of reconciliation for peace, harmony, and love
15	New Evangelization and Human Rights	Urges respect for human rights globally and on the local level

Propo-sition	Topic	Main point(s)
16	Religious Liberty	Underlines religious freedom as a "basic human right" that is unfortunately under attack at present; urges establishment of a "commission" of church officials to study the question
17	Preambles of Faith and Theology of Credibility	Acknowledges basic understandings necessary to make the new evangelization effective, such as natural law and anthropology, considered as "preambles of faith"; urges theologians to develop a "new apologetics" that will be effective in the modern context
18	New Evangelization and Means of Social Communication	Emphasizes the growth in modern means of communication and the need to use them, as well as modern languages, effectively
19	New Evangelization and Human Development	Recognizes the social teaching of the church and the connection between human development and faith
20	New Evangelization and the Way of Beauty	Connects the message of the Gospel with art and artists; emphasizes the need to capitalize on the "beautiful" and "good" in creation
21	Migrants	In the context of the ease of modern travel, recognizes migrants as both recipients and protagonists in the process of evangelization
22	Conversion	A call for personal and communal conversion, a basic element of the teaching of Jesus Christ; cites many bishops pleading for "renewal in holiness" for themselves and their people
23	Holiness and the New Evangelizers	Proposes saints as effective models of evangelization; Mary as a model of holiness
24	Social Teaching of the Church	Urges placing the church's extensive social teaching in the context of catechetics, seminary formation, ongoing formation of bishops and priests, and laity; affirms the Compendium of the Social Doctrine of the Church as a resource

Propo-sition	Topic	Main point(s)
25	Urban Scenarios of the New Evangelization	Acknowledges the unique reality of modern cities, which are so diverse, have many positive elements, but also harbor violence, crime, and corruption
26	Parishes and Other Ecclesial Realities	Acknowledges parishes and small communities as the basic place for evangelization to take hold, in union with the local bishop, but also affirms both traditional and new communities as "living cells" of evangelization
27	Education	Lists extensive ways in which education can be promoted among children, young adults in families, schools, and by teachers and educators
28	Adult Catechesis	Underlines the ongoing importance of catechizing adults in the faith
29	Catechesis, Catechists and the Catechism	Affirms catechesis as "essential" for the new evangelization; urges good use of the *Catechism of the Catholic Church* and its *Compendium*; repeats Pope Paul VI's earlier call for possibly instituting a "Ministry of Catechist"
30	Theology	Urges institutions of higher education and theological faculties, in union with the church, to make the new evangelization a centerpiece of their programs
31	New Evangelization and the Option for the Poor	Cites the church's "preferential option for the poor" to urge renewed outreach to the poor, the hungry, the homeless, the sick, the abandoned, drug addicts, the marginalized, etc.
32	The Sick	Connects the experience of sickness with Christ's own sufferings and urges sensitivity to the sick
33	Sacrament of Penance and the New Evangelization	Urges placing the sacrament of penance and reconciliation in the center of modern church pastoral activity; urges each diocese to have at least one permanent place for this sacrament with ready availability of priests
34	Sundays and Feast Days	Cites Vatican II's teaching of the Eucharist as the "source and summit" of the faith and reiterates Pope John Paul II's teaching on the importance of Sunday worship (*Dies Domini*, 1998)

Proposition	Topic	Main point(s)
35	Liturgy	Affirms the importance of celebrating liturgy well in order to foster more effectively "lifting up of hearts" to God; notes liturgy as "the best school of faith"
36	Spiritual Dimension of the New Evangelization	Highlights the "contemplative dimension" of evangelization and urges that prayer be taught from infancy
37	Sacrament of Confirmation in the New Evangelization	Urges proper and systematic catechesis of this sacrament in which the Christian receives the Holy Spirit and charisms to have the courage to witness to the faith
38	Christian Initiation and the New Evangelization	Urges reconsideration of how Christian initiation is done in diverse modern pastoral contexts
39	Popular Piety and New Evangelization	Recognizes influence of popular piety on many Catholics and urges pastoral plans to be developed to take advantage of these practices and to promote pilgrimages
40	Pontifical Council for the Promotion of the New Evangelization	Congratulates this new dicastery (Vatican office) and encourages its implementation of the synod; also urges each episcopal conference to promote the new evangelization
41	New Evangelization and the Particular Church	Recognizes how each local church (bishop, priests, deacons, laity) bears responsibility for the church's mission; urges promoting more effectively a sense of mission in each diocese or ecclesial entity
42	Integrated Pastoral Activity	Recognizes that the pastoral arena is where the main elements of faith come together; urges promotion among the faithful of personal encounters with Christ
43	Hierarchical and Charismatic Gifts	Affirms the diversity of gifts, hierarchical and otherwise, in the church; affirms the new ecclesial movements that have come into existence since Vatican II and urges them to work with dioceses and parishes in cooperative ways

Propo-sition	Topic	Main point(s)
44	New Evangeli-zation in the Parish	Urges parishes to become active "agents" of the new evangelization, reaching out to hospitals, youth centers, prisons, etc. to proclaim the Gospel message
45	Role of the Lay Faithful in the New Evangelization	Building on Vatican II's teaching, recognizes four main aspects of laity's mission: (1) the witness of their lives; (2) works of charity and mercy; (3) renewing the temporal order; and (4) direct evangelization
46	Collaboration of Men and Women in the Church	Citing their equal dignity, this proposition pro-motes cooperation of women and men on all levels of church mission
47	Formation of Evangelizers	Urges establishment of formation centers for form-ing evangelizers according to a "Trinitarian Chris-tocentricity" (making the Trinity and the centrality of Jesus Christ evident)
48	The Christian Family	Underlines importance of the family in human society and the church; recognizes sacrifices some families have made for missionary activity; recog-nizes special challenges among the divorced and remarried
49	Pastoral Dimen-sion of the Or-dained Ministry	Lengthy proposition recognizing the important role played by bishops and priests; acknowledges and regrets recent scandals; urges priests to receive ongoing formation in evangelization; urges semi-naries to focus on new evangelization with solid teaching in doctrine
50	Consecrated Life	A call to both women and men religious to make their traditions come alive; affirms "age-old tradi-tion of the consecrated contemplative life"; urges religious toward the new *aeropaghi* of mission (see Acts 17:22-32)

Propo-sition	Topic	Main point(s)
51	Youth and the New Evangelization	Recognizes youth as essential to the future and acknowledges their being influenced readily by modern media; urges capitalizing on this young audience's search for truth and meaning in life; commends World Youth Day; notes young people themselves can be "agents of evangelization," especially among their peers
52	Ecumenical Dialogue	Citing the unity found in baptism, the synod expressed gratitude for the presence of the ecumenical patriarch Bartholomew I and the archbishop of Canterbury Dr. Rowan Williams, both of whom addressed the synod; urges more ecumenical dialogues that had begun at Vatican II
53	Interreligious Dialogue	Urges ongoing dialogue with non-Christians and cooperation with them in defense of basic human rights and human dignity
54	Dialogue Between Science and Faith	Affirms both science and religion and commends dialogue between the two
55	Courtyard of the Gentiles	Promotes Pope Benedict XVI's image of the place where true dialogue can happen between Christians and nonbelievers, such as on matters of ethics, art, science, and the search for the transcendent
56	Stewardship of Creation	A call to ecological responsibility and "intergenerational solidarity"
57	Transmission of the Christian Faith	Calls all believers to renew their personal faith through a personal encounter with Jesus Christ
58	Mary, Star of the New Evangelization	Beginning with Mary's role in the church (*Lumen Gentium* 52–68), the proposition picks up on Pope Paul VI's image of Mary as the "Star of Evangelization"; she is the "Missionary" who can aid us in the new evangelization in our day

Appendix E
Lumen Fidei, Encyclical Letter of Pope Francis

On July 5, 2013, Pope Francis published his first encyclical, *Lumen Fidei* (Light of Faith), which speaks to the Year of Faith and the synod on the New Evangelization for the Transmission of the Christian Faith. The text was formally presented in Rome by Sulpician Cardinal Marc Ouellet, prefect of the Congregation for Bishops, Archbishop Gerhard Ludwig Müller, prefect of the Congregation for the Doctrine of the Faith, and Archbishop Rino Fisichella, president of the Pontifical Council for New Evangelization.

In announcing this encyclical on June 13, 2013, Pope Francis called it a document "written with four hands," noting that it had been begun by his predecessor, Pope Benedict XVI, and completed by himself. He also termed it a "strong document." In effect, it brings to conclusion a trilogy on the theological virtues originally envisioned by Pope Benedict. He had earlier published encyclicals on love (*Deus Caritas Est*, 2005) and hope (*Spe Salvi*, 2007).

The encyclical, dated June 29, 2013, on the solemnity of the apostles Peter and Paul, appeared too late to be incorporated completely into the main text of this book, but this appendix provides a convenient summary that can supplement the previous chapters.

Overview

The eighty-two-page encyclical is envisioned as the capstone of the Year of Faith and, to a small degree, a marker for the synod on the new evangelization, although another document, an apostolic exhortation on the synod, is likely to be issued at a later date. The theme of the new evangelization, as such, is barely referenced in the encyclical (see par. 42), and no mention is made of propositions from the synod. Nevertheless, there is considerable emphasis given to the dynamic of receiving and handing on the Christian faith.

One easily detects the style of Pope Emeritus Benedict XVI in the document, such as its philosophical and theological expressions, its frequent citations from Saint Augustine and other church fathers, and its treatment of the related themes of love and hope, as well as several allusions to *Porta Fidei*, which proclaimed the Year of Faith. Themes favored by Pope Francis, however, are also readily apparent, such as the use of frequent biblical imagery and attention to matters of justice and the poor. That the encyclical is an official teaching of Pope Francis was made clear at the press conference, when Cardinal Ouellet commented that "it contains much of Pope Benedict and all of Pope Francis," and Archbishop Müller noted that "we have only one pope . . . It is Pope Francis' encyclical."

The encyclical is addressed to bishops, priests, deacons, consecrated persons, and the laity. This might lead to the overly narrow view that it is solely an internally directed document, meant to enliven the faith of those already "in the fold," so to speak. An interesting aspect of the document, however, is its broader tone of respect for and awareness of those who do not embrace the Christian faith. Its global view is of the human race taken as all people (the human family) who seek the truth, who strive to achieve the best possible in life, and who are desirous of light, love, joy, and harmony in this world. It is a message for "seekers" and anyone open to greater appreciation of the truth that is knowable in this world. There is also great openness to the dialogue between faith and reason (a theme of Benedict XVI), and the desire to affirm those who, even outside the arena of Christian faith, foster peace and justice in the world. It thus has a vision of outreach to the world at large. In this sense, one can connect the message with the task of the new evangelization.

Although we cannot fully explore the encyclical here, a summary will be helpful. The chart below provides a snapshot of the encyclical, which will be followed by a few more interpretative comments.

Outline of Lumen Fidei

Section	Paragraphs	Principal Themes
Introduction	1–7	Begins with the image of "light" and God's desire to let light shine out of darkness (John 12:46; 2 Cor 4:6); faith provides the light that people seek in life and opens new pathways; sometimes faith dims, and the "light of faith" needs to be recovered; faith comes from the human desire to seek and find paths that are true; faith comes from an encounter with the living God who invites humanity into relationship, and it always opposes idolatry, which seeks to seduce believers to follow false paths
Chapter One: We Have Believed in Love (cf. 1 John 4:16)	8–22	A quick overview of the Old and New Testament presentation of faith and the history of salvation; begins with Abraham, Moses and the faith of Israel, culminating in Jesus Christ and the fullness of Christian faith, especially seen in his death and resurrection; emphasis is also given to the "ecclesial form of faith," that is, the forming of a community of faith, the church; faith is rooted in a "call" to which a response is invited
Chapter Two: Unless You Believe, You Will Not Understand (cf. Isa 7:9)	23–36	Begins with the connection between faith and truth and, using both biblical and philosophical imagery, shows how faith leads to the knowledge of truth and love; discusses faith as "hearing and sight" and how faith relates to theology and the search for God; faith is a pathway to God; also contains a section on faith and reason, showing that the two are not opposed; faith and truth go together
Chapter Three: I Delivered to You What I Also Received (cf. 1 Cor 15:3)	37–49	Using several citations from Saint Paul's letters, emphasizes the role of the church in transmitting the faith through four elements, now also expressed in the Catechism: the Creed, the sacraments, prayer (especially the Lord's Prayer), and the Ten Commandments (the Decalogue); special attention is given to baptism, confirmation, and Eucharist; defends the unity and integrity of faith as seen in the church's life

Chapter Four: God Prepares a City for Them (cf. Heb 11:16)	50–60	Broadens the perspective on faith by emphasizing how it impacts the common good, promotes the human family, gives light and life to society, and offers consolation and strength to all who suffer; the last three paragraphs (58–60) are devoted to Mary as a model of faith, as the one who "believed" God's Word to her and put it into practice; concludes with a prayer to Mary as "Mother of the Church and Mother of our faith"

Interpretative Commentary

Overall, *Lumen Fidei* is a beautiful and rather poetic encyclical letter. The blending of two papal perspectives comes across in a harmonious fashion. If one were to look for clues to new doctrinal perspectives or likely changes in the doctrinal teaching of the church here, that is not the case. This is an encyclical that is clearly in line with Pope Benedict's doctrinal vision, which is not surprising, given his role in its origin. There is, however, also a pastoral tone to the document that makes it inviting, even to those who do not share the Christian faith. It is virtually an invitation to all "seekers" and all people of goodwill who desire to know the truth and love, and to honor the deepest impulses of human identity. At the same time, the encyclical offers a deep reflection on the Christian faith expressed through baptism and fostered by celebration of the sacraments and living an authentic human existence.

There are numerous memorable lines in the encyclical. For example, using Paul's insight that "one believes with the heart" (Rom 10:10), Pope Francis emphasizes, "Faith transforms the whole person precisely to the extent that he or she becomes open to love" (26). He goes on to insist, "If love needs truth, truth also needs love. Love and truth are inseparable. Without love, truth becomes cold, impersonal and oppressive for people's day-to-day lives" (27). This focus on love and its relationship to faith harks back to Benedict XVI's earlier encyclical on love but also propels it forward to appeal to a broader audience in a pastoral way.

Most important for our purposes is the question, How does the encyclical treat the new evangelization and Saint Paul?

One of the striking features of *Lumen Fidei* from the perspective of this book is the number of times Saint Paul and/or his writings are referenced. There are more than fifty references to Paul in the text of the encyclical, and it is clear that Pope Francis greatly appreciates Paul's role in promoting the Christian faith. A Pauline citation is used in the very first paragraph (in connection with the image of light, also used in John's gospel) with the line from Second Corinthians about God shining in "our hearts" (2 Cor 4:6). The "light of faith" is not an illusory or false light but an authentic expression of the outreach of God to humanity that invites a free response.

Several other uses of Paul's letters stand out. First, for instance, Paul is cited in the context of the story of Abraham, the father of faith. Numerous passages from Paul are strung together in paragraph 11 to reinforce the image of Abraham as essential to a proper understanding of faith. Of course, it is well recognized that Paul used Abraham frequently in his letters as the great hero of faith, we might say, the one who recognized God's mysterious call and responded to it without question. Faith begins in such a vocational setting. God calls and humans respond. The document goes on to cite several passages from Paul in paragraph 15, where attention is drawn to the fulfillment of the Old Testament vision of faith in Jesus Christ, the eternal Word who is God's guarantee of love (Rom 8:31-39).

A second prominent use of Paul is citing his overwhelming acceptance of the resurrection of Christ and the new life that comes about through faith (par. 17). Interestingly, while the encyclical underlines the importance of faith *in* Christ, using a quotation from Galatians 2:20, at the same time, it explicitly draws attention to Christ's own faithfulness as God's Son. Both Christ's fidelity to the Father and our faith in Christ are important aspects of Christian faith.

Paul is also used heavily in the description of "salvation by faith" and the communal nature of this faith (pars. 19–22). This is the third example. Paul's understanding of both the individual and communal aspects of faith are thus highlighted, something we discussed in chapter 8 above. Faith comes from receiving that which is proclaimed and which invites us into union with others, who also accept the same faith. The document cites especially the famous passage from Romans (par. 22; Rom 10:5-15) about the need for evangelization in order for people to come to faith.

Proclamation demands response, and response brings one into contact with others who also respond to the call of faith.

A fourth use of Paul's theological vision is found in the image of faith as an act of both "hearing" and "seeing" (29, 37). Acknowledging the prominence of Paul's formulation of "faith coming from hearing" (Latin, *fides ex auditu*; Rom 10:17), the document goes on to connect hearing with the image of "seeing" found in John's gospel (as in John 20:8), where seeing and believing are essential, and then citing Paul again in the connection between hearing and seeing as expressed in Second Corinthians (par. 37). For Pope Francis, hearing the Word proclaimed and coming to faith by it is one aspect, but also learning to see with the eyes of faith is another. When one is transformed by faith through hearing the good news, one's vision is also changed. To use Paul's expression, one becomes a "new creation" (2 Cor 5:17; Gal 6:15; pars. 19, 41; see also par. 17 on new life in Christ).

A fifth way of using Paul's letters is found in the reference to the role of suffering (par. 57). Paul regularly recalled his multiple sufferings for the sake of the Gospel message, but he also spoke of the power of the three theological virtues—faith, hope, love—as enabling the acceptance of whatever challenges or sufferings come our way.

Finally, the encyclical invokes Paul several times on the importance of baptism in the transmission of faith (par. 41). By this first sacrament of initiation, we come into contact not only with Christ himself, in whose image we are newly made, but also with the believing community, the group of faithful whose response to the divine initiative has brought them into a familial and ecclesial relationship.

Paul is certainly not the only biblical author cited in *Lumen Fidei*, but he obviously has prominence in ways that are closely tied to new evangelization for the transmission of Christian faith, the theme of the 2012 synod. Over time, the teaching of this encyclical can and will be explored in more depth. For now we can rejoice in the gift of another teaching that sheds light on the challenge of the new evangelization in an age of skepticism and doubt.

Selected Resources for Further Reading

This list is very short and is only intended as a starting point for further exploration of the new evangelization or Saint Paul and his letters.

Boguslawski, Steven, and Ralph Martin, eds. *The New Evangelization: Overcoming the Obstacles*. New York/Mahwah, NJ: Paulist Press, 2008.

Brumley, Mark. *How Not to Share Your Faith: The Seven Deadly Sins of Catholic Apologetics and Evangelization*. San Diego, CA: Catholic Answers, 2002.

DeSiano, Frank P. *New Perspectives: A Report on the Synod on the New Evangelization* (eBook). New York/Mahwah, NJ: Paulist Press, 2013.

Dulles, Avery. *Evangelization for the Third Millennium*. New York/Mahwah, NJ: Paulist Press, 2009.

Fisichella, Rino. *The New Evangelization: Responding to the Challenge of Indifference*. Leominster, UK: Gracewing Publishing, 2012.

Hater, Robert J. *The Parish Guide to the New Evangelization*. Huntington, IN: Our Sunday Visitor Press, 2013.

Martin, Ralph, and Peter Williamson, eds. *John Paul II and the New Evangelization: How You Can Bring Good News to Others*. Cincinnati, OH: Servant Books, 2006.

Okoye, James Chukwuma. *Scripture in the Church: The Synod on the Word of God*. Collegeville, MN: Liturgical Press, 2011.

Rausch, Thomas P. *Reconciling Faith and Reason: Apologists, Evangelists, and Theologians in a Divided Church*. Collegeville, MN: Liturgical Press, 2000.

Witherup, Ronald D. *101 Questions & Answers on Paul.* New York/Mahwah, NJ: Paulist Press, 2003.

———. *Saint Paul: Called to Conversion.* Cincinnati, OH: Franciscan Media, 2007.

Wuerl, Donald W. *New Evangelization: Passing on the Catholic Faith Today.* Huntington, IN: Our Sunday Visitor Press, 2013.

Resources on the World Wide Web

http://www.usccb.org/about/evangelization-and-catechesis/. This site is the official site of the United States Catholic Conference of bishops and serves as a primary resource on evangelization. See also http://www.usccb.org/beliefs-and-teachings/how-we-teach/catechesis/catechetical-sunday/new-evangelization/index.cfm for specific resources.

http://catholic-resources.org/. This site, founded and maintained by Jesuit Father Felix Just, SJ, offers many reliable resources on Scripture, liturgy, and catechetics.

http://www.wordonfire.org/. Founded by Father Robert Barron of Chicago, this site, Word on Fire, is dedicated to Catholic evangelization and offers many different kinds of resources.

Media Resource

Catholic Update Guide to the New Evangelization: Disciples Called to Witness. DVD and CD. Cincinnati, OH: Franciscan Media, 2012. Includes leader guides for parish-level ministry. This resource may be used in conjunction with the small book *Catholic Update Guide to the New Evangelization,* edited by Mary Carol Kendzia and published by the same press.

Scripture Index

Document Index

This index indicates where church documents are either quoted or cited in the text of this book. Unless otherwise indicated, numbers refer to paragraphs in the documents, not pages.

Ingram Content Group UK Ltd.
Milton Keynes UK
UKHW020846200323
418838UK00014B/2020